W9-CDU-195

The Seven Sacred Rites of Menarche

CUMBERLAND COUNTY COLLEGE LIBRARY
PO BOX 1500
VINELAND, NJ 08362-1500

The Seven Sacred Rites of Menarche

The Spiritual Journey of the Adolescent Girl

Kristi Meisenbach Boylan

SANTA
MONICA
PRESS

RJ
145
M45
2001

05-423

Copyright 2001 © by Kristi Meisenbach Boylan

All rights reserved. This book may not be reproduced in whole or in part or in any form or format without written permission of the publisher.

Published by:
Santa Monica Press LLC
P.O. Box 1076
Santa Monica, CA 90406-1076
1-800-784-9553
www.santamonicapress.com
books@santamonicapress.com

S A N T A

M O N I C A

P R E S S

Printed in the United States

Santa Monica Press books are available at special quantity discounts when purchased in bulk by corporations, organizations, or groups. Please call our Special Sales department at 1-800-784-9553.

This book is intended to provide general information. The publisher, author, distributor, and copyright owner are not engaged in rendering health, medical, legal, financial, or other professional advice or services. The publisher, author, distributor, and copyright owner are not liable or responsible to any person or group with respect to any loss, illness, or injury caused or alleged to be caused by the information found in this book.

ISBN 1-891661-19-1

Library of Congress Cataloging-in-Publication Data

Meisenbach Boylan, Kristi, 1960-
    The seven sacred rites of menarche: the spiritual journey of the adolescent girl / by Kristi Meisenbach Boylan.
            p. cm.
        ISBN 1-891661-19-1
            1. Menarche. 2. Menarche–Miscellanea. 3. Menstruation-
-Miscellanea. 4. Teenage girls–Health and hygiene. 5. Puberty–
Miscellanea. I. Title.

RJ145 .M45 2001
612.6'62–dc21   2001040026

Book and cover design by Susan Landesmann
Cover photo © Arthur Tilley/FPG International LLC

CONTENTS

✷ ✷ ✷

APPENDIX

✷ ✷ ✷

For Amanda

"Well, this is grand," said Alice.
"I never expected I should be a Queen
so soon . . . . And if I really am a Queen,
I shall manage it quite well in time."

— Lewis Carroll,
*Through the Looking-Glass:
and What Alice Found There*

ACKNOWLEDGMENTS

Many thanks to: Katie Lady Padgett and Cassie-my-other-daughter Zook; Darcy Neice and Natalie Neice; Connie Woods, Yowona Woods, Rita Smrekar and Evrita Mays, the circle of women who nurtured my adolescent spirit; and my invincible nieces Kathleen Lanning, Allison Lanning, Julie Boylan and Kelly Boylan.

Thanks also to: Jeffrey Goldman, publisher extrordinare; Rev. David McClure and Rev. Donna McClure; Mary Nelson and Kurt Meisenbach, two twin spirits, who made my own journey through menarche bearable; Karl Meisenbach, who stole my soulskin when I was ten, but has since given it back a hundred times over; my father, David Meisenbach, who brought new meaning to the expression "shockproof"; my anchor and mother, Ann Meisenbach; Amanda, Brandan and Patrick Boylan for giving me the spaces to write; and most importantly, Ruby.

"The time has come," the walrus said, "To talk of many things: Of shoes — and ships — and sealing-wax — Of cabbages — and kings — And why the sea is boiling hot — And whether pigs have wings."

INTRODUCTION
Menarche, Rituals and Moon Cycles

THIRTEEN-YEAR-OLD RUBY HAYWOOD *drug the iron tub into the kitchen and frantically began filling it with cold water. Undressing herself as quickly as she could, she slid into the makeshift washtub and prayed. She knew that cold water was often used to stop the bleeding of cut fingers and toes, and she hoped it would work this time, too. She had been "hemorrhaging from the inside out" for almost two days and she "just knew" that if the bleeding didn't stop soon she would die. She shivered in that cold, rusty, iron tub for two hours before her father came in from the fields and found her. Ruby didn't die from hemorrhaging, but she might have died of pneumonia if she hadn't been discovered.*

I love this story, not only because it shows how far we've come in educating young girls about their menstrual cycles, but because I loved Ruby. She was my great-grandmother, and she was full of tales like this about what life was like growing up female in the early 1900s. And although I certainly relish her stories, I am thankful that times have changed since Ruby was a girl. As we move into the twenty-first century, menstrual blood, though still not a topic discussed during dinner parties, is not the taboo subject of the past. Mothers not only want to take an active role in their daughter's changing bodies, but they also recognize that puberty means more than just budding breasts and monthly bleeding. And mothers aren't the only ones participating. Fathers, single and married, are also taking a more active role in their daughter's transition. The traditional one time mother-daughter "birds and bees" speech has now evolved into an ongoing succession of parent-daughter conversations on topics such as safe-sex, birth control and relationships.

Even the general semantics used to describe menstruation have evolved. For centuries, euphemisms that depicted shame and secretiveness were the norm. But as society has become more enlightened about the natural changes of a woman's body, these derogatory expressions have given way to more linear terms. Whereas the older phrases made reference to the color of the menstrual blood or the pain associated with it, contemporary terms are directly related to its cyclic nature. Words such as "menses," "menstruation" and "menarche" (the clinical term used by the medical community to define a young girl's first period) are all derived from the prefix "mene," meaning "monthly," and have, for the most part, replaced expressions like "the curse."

The revision in terms as well as the shift in parental view can both be attributed to the freedom of communication that our world is experiencing as a whole. This freedom in communication has resulted in a more widely accepted view of the female body and how it functions. Advertising through television and other mediums has brought Tampax out of the bathroom and into the living room. Feminine care products are now a fifty billion dollar industry. It would seem impossible in this day and age for a girl to not know everything about her journey through adolescence.

And yet, even with the ongoing parental conversations and revolutionary progression in the western world, there are still many vital truths that young girls are not learning. Although parents are explaining to their daughters in clear, honest terms what happens to the female body as it moves through puberty, they, along with the advertising industry, are leaving out the emotional implications of what it means to be born a woman. More importantly, they are also leaving out what happens to the spirits of young girls when they make their transition into adulthood.

The voyage from maidenhood to motherhood is one of the most momentous spiritual passages that a female will make. It is the time when she leaves behind the sacred island of her own inner world and journeys into the core of the material outer world. It is also the time when her spirit dons the layered garments of society and, in the process, often loses itself. In *Reviving Ophelia*, Mary Pipher compares adolescent girls to Hamlet's Ophelia, who, after dressing in elegant clothes to weigh herself down, drowns herself. "Like Ophelia, all are in danger of drowning," writes Pipher. "All are pressured to sacrifice their wholeness in order to be loved." Unfortunately, young girls receive little education on how to keep their spirits afloat during this tumultuous time. They have no idea how to resist the pressure to sacrifice their wholeness, and there are no lifeboats, no preventative measures, no educational diagrams in place to instruct them.

Although many cultures use coming-of-age ceremonies in an attempt to teach young girls what it means to physically and spiritually become a woman, some of these initiation rites involve methods of torture and humiliation and are far from educational or sacred. These rituals can include anything from isolation, in which a young girl is placed away from society, to purification, in which she is beaten or tortured. The most horrendous of these rites involves the mutilation of a preadolescent girl's genitals. Current estimates by the World Health Organization state that over 135 million women and girls have been affected by some form of genital cutting, and the numbers continue to grow. Initiation rites such as female genital mutilation and purification seem inhumane by western standards, but they are very deeply rooted in the societies that practice them. To simply demand that they be stopped overnight is not realistic. I do believe, however, that these types of painful initiations can be phased out by promoting positive, life-affirming rituals in their place. For spiritual ceremonies don't have to be torturous in order to be meaningful or educational. They don't even have to be uncomfortable.

In fact, rituals in the form of celebration and storytelling can have an even more powerful effect. Through storytelling and celebration, young girls can be shown that the transition of menarche encompasses more than just monthly bleeding. And they can learn what it means to be female without having their minds and bodies mutilated. A wonderful example of this can be found in a group of Kenyan women who are calling themselves "Ntanira na Mugambo," which means "circumcision through words." With the help of the Program for Appropriate Technology in Health, a Seattle-based nonprofit organization, they have introduced an alternative to the mutilation of young African woman and are now advocating this new ritual as a replacement for genital cutting. This new model of initiation utilizes singing, dancing, storytelling and voluntary seclusion in which the girls are taught about their sexual and reproductive health.

Some additional spiritual commemorations, such as the *Bat Mitzvah*, which marks the coming-of-age of 12-year-old girls of Jewish faith, Confirmation, in which a sacrament is administered to Catholics girls already baptized, and the Latino celebration, *Quincianera*, which honors 15-year-old girls, also utilize ceremony and education to mark the transition into adulthood in a more positive manner. Likewise, the Apache puberty rite, known as the sunrise ceremony, or "Naihes," though some-what more gruelling, is a very positive form of initiation that incorporates storytelling and festivities to introduce an adolescent girl into society. There are also secular coming of age traditions, such as the Debutante Ball, which honor and celebrate girls as well.

I believe that we desperately need to expand and build on these positive, illuminating rituals and celebrations in the lives of adolescent girls, not only to eliminate the painful torturous ones, but to keep our daughters from drowning. Rituals can truly become the spiritual water wings that keep a girl afloat as she makes her voyage across the mystical seas of puberty. If used in succession, these rites can also become a spiritual blueprint of sorts that parents can use to pinpoint where their daughters are in their journey through adolescence. Because they embark on their pilgrimage at different ages, girls too can use this map to chart their own way, seeing how far they've gone and how much farther they have to go.

Adolescent girls also need these rituals in order to truly understand that menarche is not just one event, but a series of events that occur as a young girl journeys from the safe cocoon of her parent's world into a world of her own. And more importantly, girls need them in order to understand that it's okay to weep and to feel lost and alone at certain points along the way. For menarche truly is a state of being neither here nor there. It is an enchanted, in-between time when a female is neither a child nor a woman. It is also a whimsical time when emotions run high and spiritual forces become more pronounced. In fairy-tale myths, the in-between, never-never-land was always mystical and obscure. It was a place where seasons stood still, and like Peter Pan and the lost boys, little girls weren't forced to act grown up.

In fact, the entire journey of menarche is much like the adventures found in Lewis Carroll's *Through the Looking-Glass*, in which Alice climbs through the mirror that hangs over her parent's fireplace and ends up in a captivating new world. Like Carroll's tale, menarche is a story about a whimsical, imaginative, transitioning girl, who upon believing in the existence of another world, decides to make the journey through a solid and yet illusionary substance to a place where she can be of service. It is a tale about the voyage over the emotional waters of puberty, and meeting up with the Humpty Dumptys and White Knights of the world. It is about traveling down the beaches and roads and through the forest. And most importantly, it is about a young woman finally receiving her crown, an emblem of completion and wholeness and perfection.

In this book, I have attempted to create a spiritual road map using the seven distinct rites that I believe mark a girl's magical transformation from maidenhood to motherhood. It is a road map that I hope parents as well as young girls can use to navigate their way through each other's worlds. In addition to the seven rites, I have also included some positive ceremonies and initiation rituals that I hope will eventually replace the outdated, painful ones such as female genital mutilation.

In describing the journey through these seven rites, I will use the terms "moon cycle" and "period" interchangeably to describe menstruation. Though often thought of as a New Age term, the phrase "moon cycle" is anything but new. Because of its paralleling 28-day cycle, our lunar sister has been linked to menstruation for centuries, and her likeness is still used in many different countries around the world to represent a woman's period. The moon's link to menstruation is more than just a physical reference to the 28-day cycle, though. Like the sun, whose association is with man, the moon has a direct correlation to the spiritual nature of a woman. The moon represents mother, goddess and all things feminine. Its roundness and fullness reflects the natural shape of a young woman's body, and its illuminating light against the dark sky portrays the brilliance of her life-giving essence. The altering face of the moon also reflects the roller coaster of emotions that often define the journey from the maiden years to the childbearing years. And I believe it more accurately defines the alchemy of an adolescent girl's body as well.

As I write this book, my own 12-year-old daughter is moving through menarche. And as she moves through this transition, I am finding that she has as much to teach me as I do her. I celebrate her days as a young maiden as I will celebrate the days of her childbearing years. I try to allow time for her to experience her rites of passage in her own way and in her own time. And though there are days when I wonder if we will make it through alive, I revel in the glorious magic of her budding womanhood.

It is my hope that when a man or woman shares these rites with a young girl, whether she be a daughter, granddaughter, niece or friend, that they will be able to pull in a little ancient magic of the maiden years for themselves.

"Now, if you'll only attend, Kitty, and not talk so much, I'll tell you all my ideas about Looking-glass House. First, there's the room you can see through the glass—that's just the same as our drawing-room, only the things go the other way."

THE FIRST RITE

Ebbing and Flowing: The Call of the Outer World

ALTHOUGH IT OFTEN SEEMS to parents like an overnight event, the transformation from Maiden to Childbearer doesn't happen instantaneously. The changes come as a result of a long and rocky pilgrimage in which a young girl leaves behind her childhood and moves out into the adult world. This voyage, which often encompasses a decade of a young girl's life, is marked in the outer world by budding breasts, pubic hair and the most obvious sign, her first moon cycle. But the inner, more spiritual nature of a young girl begins to sense the inevitable long before it becomes obvious to her parents.

Her discovery of the looking-glass world that exists just over the water, or in Alice's case, just over the fireplace, is what defines the first rite for the adolescent girl. It is her first step in her journey toward motherhood and it is what marks her last years of maidenhood.

Most often a girl will begin to feel that she is on the verge of something spectacular right around the age of seven or eight. She will not be able to put this feeling of excitement into words. But like the changing of the seasons, she senses that spring is nearing an end and that summer is just around the corner. Maybe it is the warm, tingling sensation she gets when she views herself in the mirror. Or maybe it comes from the excitement and confidence she experiences when she is recognized for her accomplishments. But whatever it is that is stirring her awareness, a young girl innately knows that something special is just about to happen.

This sudden awareness of what awaits her comes in the form of a calling. In fact, it is much like the beckoning of a friend to come out and play. It is the outer world, this time, that speaks to the preadolescent girl. And although it is boys, parents, advertising and school that eventually convince her to leave, it is nature that first lures a young girl's attention away from the security of her own inner world.

As she hears the immortal calling of the outer world, the young girl feels a certain amount of prestige. It's as though she is being invited into an exclusive club. More importantly, she senses that her presence in the outer world is not just wanted, it is urgently needed. This feeling of being needed resonates into the depths of her very soul. It touches her in a place that was rarely touched in her own inner sanctum, and it strengthens her spirit's desire to venture out.

Over time, the low, sweet bidding of the outer world intensifies, and within a year or so, a young girl's body begins to respond. Her body does this by attempting to modulate its own biorhythms with that of the outer world. As the steady beat of her parent's world pulsates stronger and stronger within a young girl's soul, her body's own metrical beat begins to rise and fall in harmony with it. This rising and falling is much like the fluxing current of the ocean. It is the cyclic ebbing and flowing of the wavelike hormones in her veins that re-creates the familiar beat of the outer world inside her. And it is the ebbing and flowing of emotions and hormones that will work together to eventually form her moon cycle.

At first, the ebbing and flowing of the sex hormones estrogen, progesterone and testosterone may seem erratic, but these three hormones are a part of a bigger network of hormones in a very orchestrated arrangement called the endocrine system. The endocrine system, which is comprised of the hypothalamus, pituitary, thyroid, parathyroid, adrenal glands, ovaries and pancreas, is also part of an even larger, more intricate arrangement—the human body. In essence, it is the ebbing and flowing of the entire anatomy that makes up the majestic dance of a woman's menstrual cycle.

The flowing of this cyclic dance occurs when the sex hormones, especially estrogen, are at their strongest. Flowing marks the highs of the journey. And like high tide, it is a very intense and exciting occurrence. It is the time when a young woman's soul produces an effervescent joy that seems to bubble up around her. It creates an abundant amount of energy, and it is the get up and go that makes a girl want to stay up all night.

The ebbing of the cyclic dance occurs when the hormones are dropping. Like the tides, it is a time of receding, of pulling back and going within. It is the intermission of the show. An adolescent girl's energy declines during this period and her parents find that she often wants to sleep till noon. Crying and whining and a few other not-so-pleasant behaviors occur on a regular basis. But ebbing should not be thought of as an unpleasant part of the journey; a young girl needs time to go within and rethink the direction in which her life is moving. And she needs this time to plan her next steps. It is also important for a young girl and her parents to remember that ebbing and flowing go hand in hand. One without the other makes for an incomplete beat.

Although at some point the rising and falling of hormones will occur in predictable 28-30 day cycles, when a young girl first begins to hear the call of the outer world, the ebbing and flowing will be in much longer cycles. Sometimes a girl will experience four to six months of flowing, in which everything seems right with the world. She may then have a month or two of ebbing, in which she is more tearful and reflective. Or she may have three months of flowing and one month of ebbing. Once a girl has her moon cycle, the ebbing and flowing will become attuned with her menstrual flow, with the flowing coming the first half of her cycle and the ebbing the last half. But even after a young girl's first period, it often takes a year or so before she reaches a predictable 28-30 day pattern.

By the time a girl first hears the calling of the outer world and begins to respond with her own inner beat of ebbing and flowing, her parents have probably prepared her with the basics of what will happen to her body as she moves through puberty. But often parents neglect to prepare their daughters for the emotional roller coaster caused by the surges of hormones. This emotional roller coaster, which is powered by the rise and fall of hormones, is like most roller coasters. It is always exciting to watch when you are looking at it from steady ground. But the moment you are strapped in and the wind hits your face for the first time, your opinion begins to shift. Your stomach tightens, you grip the seat for balance, and hope that things don't get too rough. This emotional roller coaster is also a lot like riding the waves. Holding onto a surfboard seems okay as long as the waves are not very high. But the problem is that the journey through menarche has frequent tidal waves.

That's why it is so important for the guardians and parents of a young girl to make sure that she has all the safety belts, life rafts and other protection devices available to her during this first rite, *before* she sets out on her voyage. For the ebbing and flowing of estrogen in a woman's body is synonymous with mood swings, alternating periods of energy and fatigue, and spiritual highs and lows. And as the rise and fall in hormones over the next four to five years begins to peak, the ups and downs become very dramatic.

Thankfully, at the onset of the voyage, hormones are only released in tiny amounts, and the ebbing and flowing is relatively mild. There is still plenty of time for parents to prepare their daughter for the spiritual and emotional modifications as well as the physical ones. Typically, a young girl will ebb and flow in a smooth and rhythmic pattern for approximately a year or two before any noticeable mood swings begin to surface. This is often a peaceful and enjoyable time in the relationship between parent and daughter. The young girl is old enough to hear the faint call of her parent's world, and yet she has not been overtaken by the tidal waves of emotion that will sweep her away from her inner world. It's almost as if she can truly see and understand her parent's life without being a part of it.

Although it is never too late for a young girl to be warned of the jagged edges of the outer world, the beginning of this first rite is truly the best time to begin a series of conversations with her about her body. A young girl is still open to her parents at this time, and is often eager to put a name to what she is sensing.

In initiating these series of talks, it is best if both parents are able to sit down with their daughter and provide basic information on the female anatomy together. A unified front by both sexes reinforces the fact that the female body, and how it functions, is not something to be embarrassed about. If, for whatever reason, it is not possible for both parents to unite on these early conversations, fathers and other male role models should still play an active role in sex education with follow-up discussions. The initial dialogue, and any follow-up discussions, should include the structural layout and names of the female sex and reproductive organs, and also a little about each of the sex hormones and the effects they have on a woman's moods.

Although most public schools provide a basic sex education video/speech around fourth or fifth grade, it is vital that parents begin their own conversations with their daughter long before then. By the time a girl has reached fourth, or even third grade, she has probably already heard the sexual innuendo and street language that is associated with intercourse. Hearing about sexual relations from friends while parents are keeping mum about it, puts the whole concept in a negative light. Making a point not to speak on any given subject has a way of making it seem taboo and or mysterious. And taboo and mysterious are not the opinions that any young girl should have about sex. This does not mean that parents should relate everything they know about the subject all in one sitting, however. Although seven and eight year old girls are able to understand the concept of intercourse, they are usually not mature enough to understand other sexual practices.

The real trick comes in knowing how much information a young girl is ready to hear. Although some psychologists recommend waiting until a child asks about sex to begin the talks, I believe that by that time it is way too late. If a girl asks, that probably means that she has been thinking about it for quite some time. It is best for parents to try and stay one step ahead of what they think their daughter is ready to understand. They should start with the basic anatomy of a woman's body and then move on to the anatomy of men. Of course, most girls will have already noticed the more obvious anatomical differences and parents will, by this time, have probably answered their daughter's questions about these differences. But by bringing the topic up again and again, parents will be able to keep the lines of communication open. Additionally, they can use this reference to their daughter's changing body as a springboard for a more detailed discussion.

Another strategy is for a parent to relate his or her experiences and the experiences of other females in the family. For example, a mother might casually state, "I started to get breast buds right about your age." Her daughter will then of course asks what breast buds are. The mother will then have a springboard to talk about breast development, bras, etc. I have related my experience of starting my first moon cycle to my daughter more times than I can remember. And I have also begun incorporating "the first period stories" of other willing female friends and family into the conversations. I do this by asking a woman, who I know will be comfortable with the subject, in front of my daughter if she remembers where she was when she had her first menstrual cycle. This woman nearly always remembers this sacred event, and my daughter, though pretending not to be too interested, always listens. I have yet to see her get up and walk away.

Although parents might want to wait until their daughter is passing through the second rite to give a detailed description of hormones, if their daughter is already beginning to have mood swings, parents should bring up the subject as soon as possible. Since hormones were first discovered, there has been an ongoing controversy about what, if any, affect they had on the brain. However, in the last few years, scientists have been able to clearly show that they do indeed have a significant impact on the emotional as well as physical well-being of a woman. One of the best books I have read on the subject of hormones and how they affect a woman's moods is Gillian Ford's *Listening to Your Hormones*. This book takes an intricate look at all of the hormones, including the sex hormones estrogen, progesterone and testosterone, and explains how they influence the brain as well as the body. Although I won't go into as much detail as Ms. Ford does in her book, I will give an overview of the three basic sex hormones and their functions.

Estrogen, which is of course the most talked about hormone, is the most abundant of the sex hormones. It is made primarily in the ovaries, and it is also produced from androgens in the fat cells and adrenal glands. It is more plentiful during the first half of the moon cycle, and though still present during the last half, it tends to wane as a woman gets closer to her period. Spiritually speaking, it is the juice of God's spirit that resides in every cell of a young woman's body. And it is the moist dew that refreshes her when she lives in the outer world.

Progesterone, although considered a secondary hormone, is just as important to the ebbing and flowing of a woman's body. Progesterone gets its name from the word "gestate," which means "to bring forth." Anatomically speaking, it is the hormone that is present only in the second half of a woman's moon cycle. It is what prepares her uterine lining for the fertilized egg, and it is what keeps the lining intact while the baby is growing. Spiritually speaking, progesterone is the hormone that sustains the creative Goddess force in a woman's body. It is the calming hormone that relaxes and readies the womb to give birth to God's ideas (or children). It is the slow song that begins playing halfway through a woman's cyclic dance. At the end of the dance, if a woman has not conceived, the progesterone levels come to a crashing halt. This drop in progesterone and estrogen brings about the shedding of her uterine lining and menstrual flow. Progesterone is also a precursor to estrogen, which means it can be converted into estrogen if needed.

Testosterone is found in higher amounts in men, but it is also a very important hormone in the female body. Anatomically speaking, it is what increases the libido in a young woman. It is also a major cause of acne in teenagers. Spiritually speaking it is the get up and go that moves a young woman through her cycle, and it is the steady beat of the drum that keeps the rhythm of the other hormones in tune.

The conductors of the cyclic ebbing and flowing dance are the hypothalamus and the pituitary, two tiny glands that are located in the limbic area of the brain. The hypothalamus is the gland that puts out the releasing hormones that, among other things, tells the pituitary gland when to start the dance. The pituitary gland then sends out stimulating hormones (called "follicle stimulating hormones" or "FSH") that actually start the music playing. Once the music has started, the outward beckoning begins.

Once parents are sure that their daughter has a basic understanding of her anatomical structure, they can introduce the concept of ebbing and flowing. Most young girls are quite relieved to hear a formal explanation about the rising and falling of their hormones. They know that something is different about the way that they feel as they begin their voyage through menarche, and hearing that their ever changing moods are, in fact, quite normal, lowers their anxiety. The most important thing for girls to understand about the concept of ebbing and flowing is that flowing occurs during the first half of their cycle, and ebbing during the second half, just before their period.

It is also important for young girls to recognize that the ebbing can become quite intense as they near the time for their first moon cycle. They need to understand that this ebbing is the body's way of slowing them down and allowing them to take time to nurture themselves. Once a girl recognizes when she is ebbing, she will be more apt to slow herself down, before her emotions take over and force her activities to a screeching halt. It is equally important for her to recognize the flowing time, as this is when it is okay for her to push herself a little harder. This is the time when she can step up to the plate and accomplish her goals in the shortest amount of time.

Although in the beginning it is hard to tell that the outward has begun to call and that a young girl has begun to respond to the call, it is not long before the ebbing and flowing in her veins and in her soul begin to become quite evident. One of the most obvious signs would be the mood swings and temper tantrums that accompany the highs and lows. But even then it is hard to know just how far along a young girl is in her first ritual, because some girls are much more sensitive to the calling than are others.

Another sign is that, as the calling becomes louder and more pronounced, a young girl begins to feel quite uneasy. This uneasiness comes from having one foot planted firmly on the ground of her inner world, and the other dangling just over the water. Or it can also be symbolized as a young girl's body facing toward her inner world, while her head is turned around, straining to hear the beautiful music from the outer world. In either case, it is clearly an uncomfortable position. Not painful, yet, but definitely uncomfortable.

The most apparent signal that a girl is feeling uneasy is her inability to make decisions. A young girl who is beginning to feel the call of the outer world automatically knows that a decision will have to be made sooner or later as to whether she should follow the sound of the calling. To stay safe in the inner world of her own being, or to venture out into the unknown, and often scary, territory of her parent's world, is a difficult decision. Of course, the music and the calling will become so loud, and the ebbing and the flowing so pronounced, that the girl will eventually be washed out to sea. But for now the decision of what to do next is often torturous. This fear of making decisions carries over into her inner world. Suddenly everything from picking out what to wear to deciding what show to watch becomes a major dilemma. At this stage in the ritual, no decision is ever minor.

One of the most obvious physical signs that a girl's body has responded to the outer world is extra body fat. This fat is different from the baby fat that she may have been carrying. The plumpness this time encompasses her hips and thighs, which often seem to "curve out" overnight. The padding of her hips and thighs is an indication that estrogen has begun to reach significant levels. This rounding of her body is also a rounding of her soul, as it begins to take in and sort out the sight, smells and tastes of the beckoning outer world.

Breast buds are another anatomical sign that estrogen has began to flow. Breast buds are the tiny, knot-like bumps that begin to form under the areola (nipple) during this first rite. Though it is often hard to tell by looking at a young girl whether or not she has developed them, they can be felt. Many girls, and even a few parents, who do not know about breast buds, will panic and make an unnecessary stop at the doctor's office only to be reassured that the knots are simply the first signs of developing breasts. It is not unusual for a young girl to have a bud on one breast and not the other. Eventually, both buds will grow.

In addition to the anatomical signs that a young girl is responding to the outer world, there are also many emotional and spiritual guideposts that mark the way. The most obvious indication that a girl is responding would be the return of temper tantrums. Most children get over heavy duty tantrums by the age of three or four, and stay emotionally coherent under stress until early adolescence. For boys the first signs of impending adolescence usually start appearing around ten or eleven, but for girls, the voyage begins as early as eight or nine.

During this time it is helpful for parents to remember that tantrums, though quite embarrassing, are really nothing more than just emotional meltdowns. This means that the young girl has simply overdone or overstretched her emotions. There is a Greek word, "teinein," which means "to stretch out," and that is exactly what a tantrum is. It is a stretching out of the body, mind and spirit as the young girl moves from one stage of her life to the other. When she was two, she had little mastery over her language skills. At nine, she again finds that she does not have the words to describe what is happening to her. If you ask a two year old what is wrong when she is in the middle of a tantrum, she won't be able to answer. And the same goes for a transitioning girl. Only this time her parents are probably a little less understanding of her inability to communicate her feelings with words.

Most of the tantrums a girl has about this time result from her desire to carve out a niche for herself within the family. As she moves on to the next several stages, or rites, of menarche, she will want to establish her home base in the outside world. But for now she will explore and try to define what she is to the people she lives with. This need to define her place in the family often results in problems with her siblings, who many times are caught up in the same quest to define their own status. It is important at this time for parents to reassure their daughter of their love for her before, during and after the emotional meltdowns. And it is equally important for parents not to take these tantrums, which can sometimes turn into emotional attacks as the young girl struggles to put her feelings into words, too personally.

Of course, this is often easier said than done. After all, parents have their own emotional issues to deal with. But, like the understanding and nurturing she received as a two year old, a transitioning girl can benefit a lot from simple tolerance. And like the preventative measures that parents took when she was a toddler, it pays off in the end if parents can try and foresee any major emotional pitfalls before she gets to them. It is important to plan ahead, and at the same time keep in mind that no matter how sweet or charming a nine-year-old seems one day, the emotional climate can change at any moment.

Anxiety is another emotional guidepost that lets parents know that their daughter is embarking on this first rite of menarche. The majority of anxiety that comes at this time is a result of the initial calling of the outer world. A young girl hears the calling, but like the strange noises she hears at night, she is afraid. Although her curiosity is peaked, and she feels excited knowing that her life is about to change, she is also unsure where the calling is coming from, and what will be required of her. At this point in the first rite, she may feel strange, out of sorts, and sometimes down right panicky about the beckoning. Her body is beginning to feel a stronger pull from the ebbs and flows that are moving through her veins, and her anxiety builds as these tides build. Most of what a preadolescent girl needs at this time is lots of reassurance. It is important for her to understand that she is normal. In fact, it is instrumental that parents and guardians make sure that she understands that what she is going through is what many girls her age are experiencing, whether they admit to it or not.

Excessive clinging is another sign that a girl has begun to ebb and flow. Separation anxiety is something that children of all ages experience periodically throughout their childhood. The inability to separate at this time is related to the anxiety that she is experiencing in leaving her inner world. This is a girl's last chance to have her feet firmly planted in childhood, and it is her last chance to experience the parent-child bond before moving into puberty. When my own daughter moved through this rite, I remember thinking that some unknown trauma must have befallen her. I kept questioning her about school and friends in an effort to find out why she, all of a sudden, had to be by my side every moment of the day. There were often times, I'm ashamed to say, when I grew frustrated with her adhesion to me. This inseparability rarely lasts for more than a year or two, and if I could go back and revise my own attitude toward what I considered her errant behavior, I would. I would welcome her neediness and attentions, and would not be so quick to shoo her on her way. I would allow her sit on my lap, and to cry and to cling, until she had received enough assurance to stand up on her own.

As a young girl moves through this first rite, she also becomes more inquisitive about the divine. She begins asking questions about her parent's religion. Her questioning takes on a deeper, more philosophical tone. She wants to hear details, and she wants reassurance that her parent's faith is strong. She is no longer content to know that God lives in heaven. She wants to know where exactly heaven is and what a soul is made of. She ruminates quite frequently on the answers her parents give her, and like pieces to a puzzle, she examines their validity and size to make sure that they all fit together in the correct pattern. This pursuit of the divine and the need for reassurance is a direct result of the calling of the outer world. The transitioning girl hears the beckoning of a world that is different from the one that she is accustomed to. Suddenly she feels confused as to why she is hearing a different melody.

This pursuit of the divine also takes on a somewhat morbid quality as a girl begins to ponder her own mortality. The subject of death becomes even more uncomfortable to answer than the questions about God. Parents may be unsure of how much information to share with their daughter and seek help through books or spiritual leaders. And while sharing books on one's faith, or asking a minister or rabbi to speak with a young girl can be helpful, I still believe that nothing is quite as effective as the open and honest parent-daughter talk. Girls need to hear about the nature of death from their parents, even if it means having their parents share their own uncertainty about it.

In general, this first ritual of menarche is about the call of the adult world and the effects this calling has on the soul as well as the body of a young girl. The most important thing that parents can do at this time is to recognize that their daughter has begun to hear this call, and to prepare her spiritually and physically for her journey over the emotional waters and into the adult world by speaking with her as openly and honestly as possible.

☺ ☺ ☺

*"It was getting dark so suddenly that Alice
thought there must be a thunderstorm
coming on. "What a thick black cloud
that is!" she said. "And how fast it comes!
Why, I do believe it's got wings!"*

THE SECOND RITE
The Emotional
Waters of Puberty

AS THE EBBING AND FLOWING INTENSIFIES, and
the beckoning call of the outer world grows louder,
the preadolescent girl begins to inch closer and
closer to the shoreline of her enchanted, inner
world. This attraction to the waters of puberty is a
direct result of her desire to be a part of the adult
world. She is no longer content to just hear about
the comings and goings on the other side of the
ocean; she wants to be an active participant there.
And the closer she gets to the banks, the stronger her
yearning becomes.

The desire to find out for herself what lies on the
other side becomes overwhelming somewhere

between a girl's ninth and eleventh birthday, and she wades out into the water. The mystical sea that separates the inner-and-outer worlds of a girl's life symbolizes expansion and renewal. Paradoxically, it also represents emotion, confusion and turmoil. Water has historically been tied to initiation and purification rituals. And in the case of the preadolescent girl, the ocean water represents the painful challenges she must sail through on her voyage to the adult world, as well as the emotional depth she will achieve in getting there.

The preadolescent girl senses that the ocean is indeed very deep and the currents strong, and she knows that she will need to muster every bit of strength she has if she is going to survive the journey to the adult world. This strength will come in the form of a barge that she fashions for herself out of memories and experiences and her own inner awareness. In essence, this ethereal lifeboat that she molds is a true reflection of her confidence, her stamina and her ability to stay afloat in even the most emotional situations. And although her parents may encourage her with stories and companionship, the vessel itself must be made by her own two hands.

This is the time, when she is in the process of erecting her barge, that parents must insure that their daughter has available to her all the things that she will need to survive the rough waters ahead. Once a girl has stepped into the boat and pushed off from the dock, it will be almost impossible for her to hear the directions that are being shouted to her by her parents. One of the best ways to insure that she has the survival skills and the necessary items to stay afloat during puberty is through storytelling.

Storytelling is truly a lost art. Most parents read or tell bedtime stories to their preschoolers, but very few do this once their children have learned to read on their own. And that is tragic. Even adults enjoy hearing a good tale now and then. Stories, especially those based on their parent's adolescent experiences, have an enlightening effect on boys and girls alike. In fact, I have found that children of all ages are eager to know that Mom and Dad had an equally hard time navigating the murky waters of puberty. Fables, allegories, legends and other fictional tales that are geared toward teenage experiences and problems can also be an effective way to send a message. Storytelling is also a way of keeping the lines of communication open during a very tumultuous and often secluded time.

In my book *The Seven Sacred Rites of Menopause*, I included the story, titled "Sealskin/Soulskin," that is, I believe, one of the best allegories for women of all ages. Although it is an ancient legend, I first read it in Clarrisa Pinkola Estes' insightful book *Women Who Run With the Wolves*. The story is about a sealwoman who has her sealskin stolen by a lonely fisherman. The fisherman promises to give it back to her if she will live with him for seven years. The sealwoman agrees, and goes home with him. During the seven years, the woman and the man make a child, and the woman, though content enough with her life, becomes increasingly uncomfortable living in the outer world. Her skin becomes dry and parched, her eyelids start to peel, her hair starts to fall out. One night the child awakens to his parents arguing. It has been seven years and the sealwoman is demanding to have her sealskin back. "I want what I am made of returned to me," cries the sealwoman. The husband refuses to give his wife her sealskin back, for fear that she will leave him. The child goes back to sleep but awakens later in the night to the sound of the wind, and goes out into the dark. He comes upon his mother's sealskin and returns it to her. The sealwoman pulls on her sealskin, grabs her child and heads for the ocean. She breathes into the child's mouth three times and then dives deep into the waters. Together they swim until they are home with her family.

In this tale, the sealskin symbolizes the sacred, innermost part of a young woman. It represents her soul, her integrity and her feminine power. In essence, it personifies all that she is. And when she allows the fisherman to steal it, she gives up all that she is to the outer world. By the time the sealwoman realizes what has happened, it is too late. She must then spend the next seven years of her life trying to earn back what she already owns, and even then, it is a struggle to reclaim her soul. I have heard other women talk about the relationship between sex and the sealskin. But truly the sealskin is not about sex or virginity or even boys. A young girl's sealskin can be stolen by well-meaning friends, teachers and family members who are caught up in the outer world. It can also be divided up and given away to more than just one person. And although sexuality may reflect a certain section of the pelt, the sealskin in its entirety symbolizes the invincible spirit with which adolescent girls are born. The sealskin depicts the confidence, self-reliance, courage, determination and grace that comes with being female. It also represents the warmth and kindness and generosity that comes with being human. It is truly about a young woman's ability to be moist, strong, fearless and gentle all at the same time.

In *The Seven Sacred Rites of Menopause*, I also wrote about how hard it is for menopausal women to retrieve that part of themselves that they gave away when they were young. One reason the sealskin/ soulskin is so hard to reclaim is because women don't have a name for what it is that is missing from their lives. They have no phrase that describes the absence of their spirit. All they know is that something is missing. Another reason women find it so hard to recover their spirits is that the fishermen who have stolen their soulskins rarely offer to give them back. The fisherman in the original tale hung onto the woman's sealskin because he was afraid. The fishermen in a young girl's life do it out of fear, too, but they also do it out of selfishness and greed. They may even do it out of a misguided attempt to love. But whatever their motives, once they have that piece of a girl's soul, they hang onto it for dear life. And women who are eventually able to retrieve their soulskins often have to pay a heavy price. That is why it is so much easier for a girl to hang onto what she already owns, rather than to allow it to be taken from her and then have to spend the next several decades of her life trying to retrieve it.

And how does a girl lose her soulskin? More often than not it is given away when she unwittingly puts a higher price on someone else's happiness than she does her own. Many young women find that they are not happy unless they are "doing" for other people, whether that be their family, friends or coworkers. Young women, who are brought up by their parents to be the ever-gracious hostesses, often unknowingly put their spirits and confidence aside temporarily in order to make the fishermen in their life feel comfortable. Then, before they know it, they have either misplaced their soulskin or it has been given away to someone with less than honorable intentions.

Soulskins don't necessarily have to be given away, though. Many times they are taken through physical, emotional or spiritual assaults. It is believed that at least one out of every three girls has suffered some sort of spirit-shaking, soulskin-taking trauma during adolescence. For years these wounds were blamed on parents and other adults, but more and more is coming to light about the frequency of peer and sibling abuse.

Because it is the most conspicuous of the three, physical abuse is often the most noted soulskin-taking transgression. Thankfully, this type of battery, which includes hitting, pushing, shoving and any type of forced sex act, is finally getting the necessary attention it deserves from adults. The incidence of emotional abuse of adolescent girls by their peers is also starting to attract the attention of psychologists. While not quite as evident as physical abuse, psychological or emotional battering is said to be twice as high. Verbal attacks are the most obvious signs of emotional warfare, but the soulskin can also be stolen through a barrage of practical jokes, criticisms, disparaging remarks and sarcasm.

Probably the least understood, but nevertheless very real form of abuse, occurs on an ethereal level. Spiritual abuse can be succinctly described as the intentional demoralization of another through negative attitudes, beliefs and posturing, It is the evident disregard for the power and presence of feminine energy that slowly slips the soulskin off a young girl's back and into the hands of her oppressor. Although emotional and physical assaults can certainly take their toll, a subliminal attack on a girl's spirit can be just as damaging. Even more disheartening is that, because the stealing of her soulskin is done through thoughts and not actions, the theft often goes unnoticed. Many times the victim herself is not aware that her soulskin has been taken until it is too late. And many times it is done so silently and so deceptively that not even the oppressor is aware that he or she has taken it. Nevertheless, it is an abduction, and over time it can drain just as much self-esteem and self-worth out of a girl as a physical or verbal assault.

Parents need to talk to their daughters about emotional, spiritual and physical abuse, and they need to talk to them about their soulskins and the importance of hanging onto them at all costs. They also need to talk to them about how to be true to themselves and to their spirits, and how to hang on to their feminine power. And most importantly, parents need to hear what their daughters are saying. Young girls need to be heard, and they need to know that they are heard.

I remember listening in horror at the bottom of the stairs one morning as my 11-year-old daughter, through a flood of tears, practically broke the sound barrier in an effort to get me to hear her. I had been on her for quite some time about how she should put more effort into getting along with her younger brother. She had told me that morning, as she often had, that her brother was bothering her. As usual I had brushed her off by saying "just get along with him." I will never forget the energy that she had to muster to finally get the point across that his antics were just too much for her to handle. Her face was beet red and her shoulders were thrown back in defiance as she screamed down to me from the top of the stairs, "You are NOT hearing me! I can't TAKE IT anymore!" I finally heard her that morning, as I'm sure had most of the neighbors, and I took immediate steps to correct the situation. But it is a scene that will forever stay in my mind on what it takes for an adolescent girl to get her mother's attention.

In her book, *A Woman's Worth*, Marianne Williamson writes that as women we "are still in emotional bondage as long as we have to make a choice between being heard and being loved." Up until that morning on the stairs, I had unwittingly been giving my daughter a choice—be heard or be loved. I had ignored her feelings and insisted that she compromise her right to be left in peace in order to please me. In this case, I was the one putting her in bondage. I was the fisherman slowly slipping the soulskin off her back. Today, I make it a point to listen, to really listen, to what she is saying. And I make it a point to let her know that her voice doesn't have to reach such decibels in order for her to be heard or loved.

It is important that parents make sure that their daughter knows that she is heard and loved, and that she is aware of the value of her soulskin, *before* she sets sail to the outer world. Many girls are not even aware of the power of their feminine spirit. I know I wasn't. And if a girl is not aware of the intrinsic worth and uniqueness of her soulskin and her voice before she leaves her enchanted island, then chances are good that she will give these priceless pieces of her spirit away without ever knowing their value. For once on the boat, a young girl will often get so caught up in the excitement of the new and exciting experiences ahead that she will lose track of all that was important to her in the inner world. Or she will be so lonely for companionship from having spent the years on her barge, that once she arrives in the adult world, she will give away her spirit and her voice to the first person who comes along.

I have shared the poignant story of the soulskin, and the allegory of how it gets lost or stolen, with my daughter and her friends many times over the years. I believe it is one of the truest legends that I have ever heard, and I believe it is a story that women of all ages should hear. And there are many other tales like it out there that parents can use to inspire their daughter on her voyage across the seas.

In addition to telling her stories and reminding her to hang onto her soulskin, there are other ways parents can prepare their daughter before she steps onto her barge. One of the best floatation devices a parent can provide is a positive outlet for her emotions. Sports have always been a great conduit, not only for excessive physical energy, but for emotional energy as well. In decades past, girls were rarely encouraged to play sports past puberty. It was thought to be unladylike and bad for a girl's image to be competitive. Furthermore, menstruating girls were discouraged from physical activity during their moon cycles on the grounds that it would cause excess bleeding and cramps. Today we know the opposite is true. In fact, the Women's Sports Foundation reports in a recent study that girls who play sports wait longer to become sexually active, are more likely to use contraception and are less than half as likely to get pregnant as are girls who are nonathletic. Staying active before, during and after the menstrual cycle also lessens physical discomfort and brings about a stronger sense of well-being throughout the month.

Although some girls who were very athletic as preadolescents find their attention waning as they near the time to step on the barge, it is important for parents to continue to encourage and promote physical activity, whether that be in organized sports or through other mediums, such as dance or cheer-leading. To do so will not only inspire a sense of physical well-being, but will foster spiritual and emotional stability in their daughter as well.

Another emotional outlet for young girls comes in the form of writing. Whether journaling in a diary, or composing a poem or song, putting words and thoughts to paper is one of the best ways to release suppressed emotions. I can't help but think that is why graffiti is so popular among young people. There is something very liberating that happens when feelings are materialized on paper, or the side of a house for that matter. I remember copying my boyfriend's name over and over in every different writing style imaginable when I was in seventh grade. In fact, I still have one of my diaries in which 24 pages are filled up with this boy's name. Today, I can't even remember what this young man looked like. But at 13, with emotions and hormones raging, this was the best, and probably safest, way to release my overflow of emotions. And love isn't the only emotion that gets released through the written word. Anger, hate, resentment, and other not so pleasant feelings can also be expressed. On many of the pages of this same diary were the words "I hate Mom" recorded over and over. There were also a few choice words that I wouldn't have been caught dead saying aloud, even if I were by myself.

This is also the time, *before* she sets sail, that parents need to make sure that their daughter is aware of all the social, physical and spiritual ramifications of having sex. It is hard to live in our society and not know about the AIDS epidemic, and yet young people are regularly having sex without proper protection. Psychologists say that this is because young people often fall into the "it won't happen to me," or the "it won't happen to me if I just do it once" mode of thinking. For decades this is what sent teenage pregnancy skyrocketing. Now that the stakes have increased and sex has truly become a matter of life and death, it is imperative that young women and men know how to take care of their bodies. And whatever their own personal views are about premarital sex, parents still need to prepare their daughter, because we all know that hormones tend to take on a life of their own during the adolescent years.

Preparing a young girl means making sure that she understands that it only takes one time to change her life forever. It also means teaching her the importance of thinking and planning ahead. One way of helping her to do this is to role play with her, and have her come up with solutions on how she will handle difficult situations. It is equally important to make sure that she understands that adult assistance is available to her, no matter what choices she decides to make.

Parents should also make sure that their daughter understands the facts about conception. Despite sex education, many teenagers, and indeed many adults, still fall victim to the "a woman can't get pregnant if she, or when she" myths. The fact is that a young woman who has ovaries and has started her period can get pregnant at any time, anywhere and in any position. (In fact, a young woman can get pregnant up to a year or so before she actually starts her period. This is an even greater reason for parents to prepare their daughter early on.)

Taking care of her body isn't the only thing a young woman needs to know when it comes to sex. Taking care of her heart and spirit is equally important. Girls (and boys) need to understand that having sex is more than just a physical act, it is an act of the spirit. It is a joining of the souls and it is an opening up of the most vulnerable part of themselves. Again, it is essential that parents reiterate the story of the sealskin/soulskin and how important it is to hang onto it. Far too often, when a girl gives away her body, her soulskin goes right along with it.

After a girl has finished constructing her barge, and hopefully understands all the ramifications of what lies ahead, she is ready to begin her journey. It is at this point that she must make an active decision to step onto the boat and wave farewell to the magical, inner world of childhood. As she pushes her boat away from the shoreline, she is, in essence, pushing herself away from her parents as well. She must do this in order establish her independence. And more importantly, she must do this in order to re-create her identity as an adult. When a girl actively pushes away from her parents, rather than having them nudge her off the island, she is signaling to the world that she is able to act and think for herself, and she is signalling to her parents that she is strong enough to face the rough waters on her own.

There are many different ways in which a journeying girl propels herself away from the shoreline. One of the most obvious ways is through negative behaviors. By acting in a contradictory man-ner, a girl puts emotional distance between her and her parents. This feeling of distance and isolation then enables her to turn her attention toward the outer world. Although it is certainly frustrating for parents who have to put up with a defiant and disobedient daughter, it is important to remember that this ritual of catapulting herself from the safety of her inner world is just as frustrating and frightening for the journeying girl.

Another not so pleasant sign that a young girl is attempting to push away from the shoreline is an increase in her backtalk. Many parents feel that backtalk is a sign of disrespect and should not be tolerated. But a girl who is rudely talking back to her parents at this time in her life is usually doing so out of a growing sense of independence rather than irreverence. Again, it is just another indication that she is attempting to expel herself from the shoreline of her inner being. She is talking back to her parents in an attempt to create distance, and she is talking back in an effort to create autonomy for herself.

In addition to creating emotional space, many times a girl will literally create physical space between herself and her parents. She is no longer interested in participating in family activities, and she wants to spend a lot more time with friends. I believe this is one of the hardest times for parents. Letting go of something that is so treasured and so loved is never easy. And a parent is right in thinking that there are a lot of atrocities that await their daughter in the middle of the water, as well as in the outer world. But the consequences of not letting a girl embark on her journey are even greater.

To keep a young girl locked in her own inner world forever is simply not possible. She will eventually leave the island one way or another. And when parents attempt to retard her voyage, it often forces a girl to further rebel by violently propelling herself away from the shore. They also risk building a wall between themselves and their daughter that could take years, and even decades to tear down. Encouraging a girl to embark on her journey does not mean that parents should allow her to totally disconnect from them for good, however. It just means that the silver chord between the two should be given a lot of leeway. And if they haven't already, parents should develop a loud and strong voice. The adolescent girl will often be in need of direction as she floats in the middle of the lake, and it will take some incredible lung power from her parents in order for her to hear them.

As she gets further away from the shoreline, the strong currents of the mystical sea sweep over her barge and, like tides against the tiny grains of sand of her inner being, propel her even further toward the outer world. Once afloat in the middle of the lake, a girl's body becomes quite uncomfortable. She is no longer grounded in her inner world, nor is she grounded in the adult world. She is, in essence, caught between two worlds. This second rite is truly the pinnacle of being everywhere and at the same time being nowhere. During this ritual, which often lasts a year or two, the journeying girl is caught up in emotional issues of all kinds. Voyaging through unfamiliar territory, she is in a heightened state of awareness. This foreign state brings about extreme sensations and her emotions tend to run the gamut. She becomes more passionate about environmental and political issues, and quickly angered by what she sees as injustices. She cries when she's sad, she cries when she's angry and she cries when she's happy. And since there is no middle ground during this rite, it means she's pretty much crying all the time.

It is important for a girl to eventually learn to harness her tears and emotions, and at some point along her menarcheal voyage she will do just that. But for now she must be allowed to experience them fully. These emotions, in part, are what power her barge and sail her in the direction of the outer world. Although it can be quite painful for parents and siblings to stand by and watch as the young girl works through these feelings, like all rituals, this rite must be moved through, not around. Eventually she will learn how to steer her barge, and to use her oars and all the other available sources with which her parents have provided her.

As a girl drifts in the middle of these two worlds, she begins to ponder the reality of a divine being. During the previous ritual, the preadolescent girl was spiritually consumed with a passion to know anything and everything about her parent's religious beliefs. In this ritual she has time to reflect on and question what she has learned. This questioning isn't about challenging their beliefs entirely, it is really more of a simple questioning. Whereas before she took her parent's beliefs at face value, she now begins to deliberate on how these beliefs fit into her own life. This spiritual quest at this time is not unusual, for it is during the loneliest times of our lives that we question our faith. And for now, this is truly a lonely time for the preadolescent girl. She is, for the first time in her life, emotionally adrift from her parents and family. She is alone in the emotional waters of two worlds.

*At the next peg the Red Queen
turned again, and said,
"Speak in French when you can't
think of the English for a thing—
turn out your toes as you walk—
and remember who you are!"*

THE THIRD RITE
The Bonds of Sisterhood

AT THE BEGINNING of this third ritual, a preadolescent girl finds that she is drifting in the waters just off the shores of her inner world. She is alone, and whether she admits it or not, very afraid. Her feet are no longer on stable ground. She is being kept afloat by her barge, her own inner strength. The ebbing and flowing of her hormones seem to be pushing and pulling her in both directions, and with each wave that crashes against her boat, she feels herself becoming more and more seasick.

No amount of warning or forethought on the part of a parent can accurately prepare a girl for the perpetual back and forth motion and resulting queasiness that hallmarks this third ritual. In a preadolescent girl's mind, the outer world is always just minutes away. And only after the days turn to weeks, and then to months, and she finds that she is still floating aimlessly in the water between both worlds, does she begin to grasp the time-span of the journey.

At first she is merely impatient at the lack of progress. She was sure that she would have been able to participate in the adult world by now. And yet, she is still neither here nor there. This feeling of restlessness quickly turns to anger, and then to outright terror as it suddenly dawns on her that her parents were right—puberty is a long and difficult voyage. This fear further grips her spirit once she realizes that there is no turning back.

A girl often becomes quite alarmed at this point in her journey, as waves of anxiety crash over her barge and into all areas of her life. She panics about schoolwork, she panics about friends and she panics about what to wear and what to eat. She even panics about the fact that she feels panicky all the time. If no one explains to her that her anxious feelings are normal, she may eventually develop psychosomatic illnesses. In the third ritual, these illnesses may start out as occasional stomach aches, but if left unchecked, they can develop into everyday occurrences that keep her from functioning normally as she enters into the fourth and fifth rituals. Daily calls from the school nurse about everything from headaches to stomach pains can easily become the norm.

It is a wise parent who sits his or her daughter down and explains to her that these anxious feelings are a normal part of the journey. It is helpful, too, if a parent can go over what symptoms a preadolescent girl can expect to feel *before* she reaches the point of panic. Many girls, and indeed many parents, do not recognize the symptoms of anxiety. In fact, many girls often end up at the doctor's office with general complaints such as "I just don't feel right." Further questioning often reveals that they have a racing heart, numbness or tingliness in the extremities, shortness of breath, sweaty palms—all symptoms of a panic attack. When a preadolescent girl begins to complain about feeling odd or out of sorts, it is important that her parents find out what she means before brushing her symptoms off. The sooner a girl is able to get a handle on her anxiety, the sooner she will learn to navigate the waters around her.

Once she is able to calm herself down, she will also find her seasickness subsiding—at least momentarily. At this point she is able to think more clearly, and she begins to reexamine her barge and her persona. If she has packed the right navigational tools, she pulls them out and begins to use them. She knows that if she is going to survive the journey, then she will have to gather all her inner strength and concentrate on staying upright in the turbulent, emotional sea that surrounds her. So she struggles to keep her wits about her as best she can, and focuses on getting to the adult world in one piece.

As a girl moves farther out, she begins to feel the power of her own inner strength and begins to act more responsibly. She is well aware that she is on her way to womanhood, and she wants to act as well as look the part. It is at this time that girls will often begin to shun the frilly dresses and other little girl attire. They will also leave behind anything they consider to be childish. Though their rooms may still be filled with dolls, their interests are turning more and more to the outside world. If they were tomboys, this phase, too, is quickly dropped as their barge drifts further out into the water.

During this ritual, preadolescent girls no longer want to pretend to be women, they actually want to look like women. And in their eyes, looking like a woman means donning makeup and heels and wearing their hair a certain way. It also means having the right clothes.

This need to have the appropriate attire is the hallmark of the ritualistic jaunts to the mall. These ceremonial excursions are a time consuming, not to mention expensive, rite of passage. And yet they define parent-daughter bonding. The quest to find womanhood amid the endless forest of seductive goods, only to come away with nothing but a frazzled parent and a belligerent child, is a tale as old as time. It is an intricate part of the push-pull connection in which the preadolescent girl continues to use her parents as springboards to move farther out across the seas.

The journey over the waters and through the malls also awakens girls to the sights and sounds of the voyagers around them. Later, as they near the shores of the outer world, they will become interested in companions as sexual partners, but for now they are only interested in those who they feel can further their journey along. And for preadolescent girls, that is usually older, more advanced forms of their own sex—teenage models, singers and other celebrities.

In fact, one of the most obvious indications that a girl is on the barge and headed for the outer world is her infatuation with female pop stars. As with all crushes, the admiration that a girl feels for these celebrities shows up in the form of imitation. Not only does she want to dress like these stars, but she literally wants to talk, walk and act like them. In addition to having crushes on celebrities, she may also be emulating more mature relatives such as older sisters, cousins and aunts, or neighbors, teachers and family friends. In fact, any woman or older girl that leads an interesting or glamorous life is fair game.

This infatuation and its ensuing imitation comes out of the indecisiveness and insecurity that a girl feels about her own changing body. She is constantly comparing herself with women she sees on television and in magazines. In essence, she is experiencing different styles and forms of behavior in an effort to better define herself. And she is exploring and trying on characteristics of other females in an effort to cultivate her life in the outer world.

Although most crushes are harmless, parents do need to make sure that these infatuations stay infatuations and don't turn into borderline obsessions. Imitation is one thing, but to actually mold one's life around someone else is another matter all together. It is imperative, for her emotional and spiritual health, that a girl retain her inner autonomy during these adolescent years, even while she is aligning her outward persona with another female. Like the loss of her soulskin, the loss of her identity is something that becomes difficult to reclaim once it is gone.

It is also important at this time for parents to be aware of the fact that their daughter is more than likely receiving an inaccurate image of what it means to be a woman. Because she is being flooded with sexually explicit images of waif-like supermodels, she is likely to feel inadequate and degraded. And nothing can capsize a girl's barge faster than the delusional images that society has of women. The best deterrent to making sure that a journeying girl does not embrace these images as truth, is to make it a point to speak out against them. A good way to go about this might be for parents to talk about how the pictures in magazines are often altered or enhanced to make the subjects look more beautiful than they really are. Parents should also point out that these models represent less than one percent of all women.

Truly the easiest way to teach a girl how important it is to love the body she was given is by being a good example. Mothers who constantly berate themselves in the presence of their daughters are only perpetuating the myth that one has to be perfect in order to be beautiful. A mother should make a point of letting her daughter see her admiring her own reflection in the mirror, and she should do it often enough for her daughter to get the point that self-admiration is a good thing.

In addition to being aware of the inaccurate images with which their daughter is being bombarded, parents should be aware of eating disorders. It is during this ritual, between the ages of 10 and 13, that girls first begin to become aware of how much or how little they eat. Over the past few years, calories and fat grams have become the favorite topic of conversation at school lunch tables. Over the counter dieting aids are now sold by the thousands to girls under the age of eighteen. Bulimia and anorexia have become common, not only among older teenagers, but among younger girls as well. And although these facts have come to the forefront, society continues to reinforce the "you can never be too thin" myth. That is why parents need to take matters into their own hands by reading up on the signs of eating disorders and being aware of their daughter's eating habits.

As girls move through this ritual of same-sex crushes they often worry about what these crushes mean. They may even wonder if their strong feelings toward another female are signs of being a lesbian. But the same-sex attraction that girls this age have is quite different than the sexual attraction that defines lesbianism. This type of same-sex attraction is innocent, uncomplicated and rather simplistic. It is not love, in the deep, meaningful way that is felt between lesbians. It is giddy and fickle and whimsical, as crushes often are. And it is short-lived. For as a girl gets closer to the shores of the outer world, these feelings of adoration often become more focused on boys.

In addition to the adoration felt for older females, an important part of this third ritual is a preadolescent girl's bond with females her own age. Friendship is a vital part of being human. Without intimacy, we cease to grow. And never is this more apparent than during adolescence. Being stranded in the waters between both worlds is difficult enough. Doing it alone is almost impossible. That is why it is essential for girls to bond with others their own age as they move toward the outer world. Preadolescent girls need the comfort that only another preadolescent girl can provide. They need someone who is just as scared, anxious, and excited as they are. And while siblings and parents and teachers can be of some comfort, there is nothing like a best friend to help navigate the waters.

For many girls, finding a few close friends to share the experience is an effortless task. But for others, especially those who are naturally shy or reserved, finding and keeping friends is not only difficult, it is quite painful. This is when parents must walk the proverbial tightrope of knowing when to step in and knowing when to step out. I remember reading a poster that listed the ten rules to being a good parent. The first rule was "stay out of your children's social lives." Generally, this is indeed a good idea. Especially when it concerns friendships that have already been established. But sometimes it is necessary for parents to intervene into the social lives of their children; especially when no social life exists. Although most preadolescent girls would be horrified at the thought, this intervention doesn't have to be obvious or heavy-handed. Often times it just takes a little planning and discreet delegation.

When my daughter, Amanda, was starting a new school, she was quite worried about fitting in. I talked with her about her anxiety and about how everyone feels nervous about joining an established group. We then discussed several ways in which she could approach the other girls in her class. I suggested a few "icebreakers," or topics of conversation that she could use to connect with the other girls. Some of these suggestions she liked, some she did not. But our conversation led her to think of her own icebreaker. The next day when she returned from school, she told me about one of the ones she used during lunchtime that got the whole table talking. It wasn't anything exceptional, this icebreaker, in fact, it was something as simple as bringing up the latest news about a pop star. However, it was said with enough confidence and finesse that she was able to get the attention of all the other girls.

In addition to assisting their daughters with new friendships, it is equally important for parents to speak with them about the art of keeping friends. Girls this age tend to team up and form cliques. Being with the popular group becomes the focus, and many times friendships then become quite disposable, depending on who is in and who is out. This is probably the most painful time of adolescence, because struggling to remain with the "in crowd" becomes more than just a past time; it becomes an obsession. There is a wonderful book out by Trevor Romain titled *Cliques, Phonies, and Other Baloney* that is directed toward adolescent girls. It addresses friendships and popularity and how girls as well as boys can better deal with cliques at school. It also includes some great advice on peer pressure.

As a preadolescent girl continues to journey across the water, she will feel as though her body is growing at an incredible rate, and indeed it is. The physical alterations that occur during this ritual are more profound than any other ritual. And while she has not quite reached her targeted height, she is definitely looking more like a woman than a girl. According to the book *All That She Can Be*, by Dr. Carol J. Eagle and Carol Colman, between the ages of 9 and 13 "the average girl will become 25 percent taller and will almost double her body weight." These changes often seem to appear quite suddenly. In fact, almost overnight the journeying girl's breasts become more than just buds, they become full. Her pubic hair fills in, and she begins to routinely shave her underarm and leg hair. During this time of rapid changes, the sweat glands kick into overdrive and hygiene becomes a major concern. In addition to using underarm deodorant, she may see the beginning signs of acne, which is caused by the increased testosterone in her system. Many parents also find that their daughters are taking longer and more frequent showers and baths.

Some emotional changes that parents can expect from their daughter during this ritual are an increase in indecisiveness as she continues to ebb and flow, and an increase in the amount of arguing. Many times mothers will take the brunt of this arguing— although I have seen a few dads take quite a tongue lashing from their daughters. This need to bicker about everything, from what to wear to what to do, takes on a painfully cutting edge during this rite. In the second ritual, a young girl may have been sarcastic, but once she leaves the inner world and moves out onto the waters, this sarcasm takes on a sharp and hostile edge. The battle of the wills is the emotional name of the game. Parents would be well advised not to dig their heels in too early or too quickly, though. If they overreact to the suddenly hostile nature of their adolescent daughter, they will find themselves battling over everything. And I mean everything. The journeying girl must use these arguments in order to propel herself across the water. If parents insist on winning each and every struggle just so they can prove who is in charge, then they may find the last connecting tie that they had to their daughter quickly severed.

It is best if parents make a list of the things they will compromise on, versus the things that they will absolutely not give in to. One of the things I never compromise on with my daughter is safety. I have made it quite clear to her that I will do whatever it takes, including climbing into her boat myself, to keep it upright. On the other hand, I could care less what she wears as long as she doesn't get arrested or thrown out of school for it. That also goes for eating and sleeping. I stopped trying to control Amanda's bedtime and table-time habits right around the time I stopped trying to control her bathroom habits. She is fully aware of the fact that when she gets the required amount of sleep, she feels much better. She is also equally aware of the fact that sugar highs are not long lasting. However, if her eating or sleeping patterns were to become a safety issue, then I would most certainly step in.

The spiritual quest, which took on a more skeptical appearance during the second ritual, begins to move in a totally different direction at this time. As discussed earlier, preadolescent girls have a propensity to identify with other females during this ritual, and so the pursuit of the Truth, like the pursuit of the outer world, becomes more female-oriented. Female archetypes, such as Aphrodite and Athena, become fascinating to the journeying girl as she rebels against the predominately male-oriented deities. Greek Mythology is an excellent outlet for girls this age who relish tales of the power of legendary goddesses. Folklore is full of goddesses and female deities. Though not all of these images are positive, they will satisfy the longing of the journeying girl to touch that divine feminine nature within her own heart.

As the young girl progresses spiritually, emotionally and physically across the waters of puberty, she begins to get a feel for what life will be like when she reaches the outer world. And while the changes that she experiences at this time may seem futile and unimportant, they are truly a vital and necessary part of becoming an adult. This ritual, like all the rituals, is a stepping stone. It is one of the many punctuations on the adolescent voyage that allows a girl to bring order to the ever-expanding possibilities that await her in the outer world.

"That accounts for the bleeding, you see,"
she said to Alice with a smile. "Now you
understand the way things happen here."
"But why don't you scream now?" Alice asked,
holding her hands ready to put over her ears again.
"Why, I've done all the screaming already,"
said the Queen. "What would be the good
of having it all over again?"

THE FOURTH RITE
The First Moon Cycle

DURING THE EARLY MONTHS of this fourth ritual, the journeying girl's barge approaches the coast of the outer world and begins to steady a bit. The ebbs and flows of the tantrum-filled emotional waters are not as pronounced, and the adolescent girl, though still somewhat shaky from the rough voyage, begins to discern her whereabouts. She intrinsically knows that dry land is inches away, and that soon her barge will harbor in the port of the adult world. The blood within her womb begins to stir, as does her excitement.

Although the echoing voice of her inner world can still be heard, in the throes of excitement at nearing the outer world, she often chooses to ignore it. Over the years, the voice of her own inner spirit will weaken until it becomes barely audible. And if she is not forewarned about the dangers of silencing it, then she may find the resonance of her inner world squelched before she has even docked.

That is why, if they have not done so already, it is imperative that parents instill in their daughter the importance of relying on her own instincts. Adolescent girls must remember to listen to their own inner voice above all others, no matter how tiny and slight that voice may be. Intuition, which is the one true weapon that cannot be taken away once it is mastered, will keep a girl safe from the dangers of the new land. If a girl is able to tap into and take the advice of her own inner spirit, and at the same time live fully in the outer world, then she will find peace and joy in both lands. She will also be able avoid many of the heartaches that await her.

As the steadfast barge approaches the shoreline, the journeying girl begins to fidget in anticipation of the imminent merger. Her eyes and her heart widen as boys and other trappings of the adult world come into focus. Never is this outer world so animated and so fascinating as it is through the eyes of an adolescent girl. The journeying girl knows that she is nearing adulthood and that soon she will be able to participate in life in ways that had previously been forbidden. Dating, autonomy and driving hang like trinkets against the landscape before her. This first glimpse that a girl gets of these frills is much like her first trip to the circus. At first she is overwhelmed by what she sees and is content to be a spectator. But then, as her spirit becomes more acclimated to the carousel of adventures, she becomes intent on being an active participant. After months of drifting just outside the shores, she finds that she has become so overstimulated that she literally cannot stay seated in her barge.

This excitement manifests itself physically through a sudden burst of development in the adolescent girl. Not only does her body experience a growth spurt, but her energy level expands to encompass the dimensions of the adult world before her. It is as though she is not only taking the new world in through her eyes, but through her body as well. As she stands poised in her barge, just outside the new world, she is able to draw adulthood into her and transform herself physically to fit what she sees before her.

This growth spurt, which typically begins about a year or so before her first moon cycle, often comes about in the summer months. Doctors say that they are not sure why children often seem to shoot up over the summer, and there is no actual scientific proof of why this happens. However, this sprouting of children, like the sprouting of wheat in the fields, often coincides with the summer solstice, when the days are long and the nights are short. I can't help but believe that it is nature's way of harvesting its own.

The anticipation of her merger with dry land also manifests itself spiritually and emotionally in a journeying girl's psyche. Even as I write this chapter, my own daughter's barge is nearing the shore. She has grown two inches this past summer, and I can see the excitement of this "harvesting" reflected in her eyes. There is a certain urgency about everything she does. Her anxiety level has reached the point that she is having a hard time sleeping through the night. As I am in menopause, and am experiencing a harvesting of my own, I am also having a hard time sleeping. Many times I find that we are up in the middle of the night together. On these nights I remind her, and myself, that this is only a stage. And that this wakefulness, this mindfulness of all that she and I are becoming, is just a part of the rites that we must pass through on our way to each other's worlds.

I also remind her that her spirit and her body are working together in making the final preparations for her first creation ritual. This creation ritual, or moon cycle, which is formally titled "menstrual cycle" by the medical community, is the way in which life expresses itself. Prompted by hormones and God's touch, it is a mixing of blood and spirit into a circular, 28-day dance that transforms the female body from a mortal figure into a divine vessel. In essence, it is the way that the Goddess in every woman creates and prepares to give life, and creates and prepares to give life again and again.

This alchemy of the menstrual cycle and its affect on the spiritual nature of men and women alike is very understated in the western culture. But it is a steadfast miracle nevertheless. And although my daughter feigns indifference when I remind her of this, I can see in her eyes that she truly revels in the glory of her divinity.

As the journeying girl's body makes its final preparations for its first moon cycle, her once perpetual excitement and wakefulness will suddenly be broken up by intermittent bouts of exhaustion. She will, maybe for the first time in her life, look forward to taking naps. Parents may also be surprised to find that their daughter, who has previously been up at all hours, suddenly going to bed at 9:00 P.M. and sleeping to noon. Spiritually, this fatigue is the result of being bombarded by the new and exciting images of the outside world. Physically, this fatigue is the result of her body being bombarded with estrogen. This intermittent exhaustion is the same type of weariness that is experienced by pregnant women during the early months of gestation when their bodies are adjusting to the increase in hormones. It is best to let the journeying girl rest whenever and wherever she can until her body gets used to the adult world, even if this means sleeping all day on the weekends.

Like the growth spurt she experienced during the early part of this ritual, the official start of a girl's moon cycle often occurs during the summer months. Like a tidal wave that is building in the warm waters off the coast, the warm blood of her uterus builds up inside her and comes crashing down in the form of her first period. At this exact moment, which often occurs somewhere between her tenth and fourteenth birthday, the journeying girl's barge intersects with the shore. This connection marks her formal initiation into her childbearing years. Her moon cycle then becomes the rope that harnesses her barge to the outer world. Her barge will stay tethered there until she reaches menopause, when she will again need its services to ferry her across the water and back to her inner world.

In the past, a girl's first moon cycle was rarely acknowledged, much less celebrated. Girls were less attuned to the changes in their bodies, and were not told what to expect ahead of time. More often than not, girls found the joining of their barge with dry land more like a crash than a merger. One day they were floating along in the water, and the next day they found themselves shipwrecked in the adult world with little if any preparation for their moon cycle. And while it is rare that a girl in the twenty-first century starts her period the way that my great-grandmother Ruby did, most girls are still uninformed and unprepared physically, emotionally and spiritually for their initiation into the child-bearing years. Often, what little, if any, anatomical facts are offered, are presented in a way that makes them seem callous and clinical. Little, if any, is said about the emotional fluctuations that the outer world brings, and the explanation of the spiritual transition is practically nonexistent. But the omission of these changes does not alter the fact that they occur. And they occur in ways that are often impossible to ignore.

Although some believe that the menstrual cycle is a simple process, the transformation that the female body undergoes during these 28-30 days is actually much more complicated than even most grown women are aware of. Because of its complexity, and the fact that menstrual blood was considered taboo for so long, many of the anatomical details of menstruation are still not discussed. Pertinent information, such as how much or how little blood actually flows, what alters the color of the flow, and what causes the lining of the uterus to build up, are often sidestepped by mothers and teachers alike. In fact, it is often said that adolescent girls know more about the life cycle of a fruit fly than they do their own menstrual cycle. I know it was true of my generation, and although schools and parents have made progress in the area of sex education, from talking with my daughter, I can see that this advancement is not nearly enough.

School officials contend that the deficiency in information is due to the lack of time. They say there is simply too much information to go over in the short span that they have allotted for the subject.

So, in an effort to keep it short (and whether they admit it or not, not so embarrassing), they limit their talks to the basics. Parents, who on the other hand have all the time in the world, simply don't know enough about the details to explain it fully. But something, or someone, has to give. Girls need to be taught everything about their body and how it works, including detailed information about their sex organs and menstrual flow. Although I hope that schools will eventually begin to devote more time and energy into teaching these subjects, for now, at least, parents must pick up the slack and educate themselves and their daughters on how the female body works. The best book around for brushing up on the subject is *Our Bodies, Ourselves: A Book by and for Women from the Boston Women's Health Book Collective*. This manual, which has been around for over 25 years, has recently been updated and expanded, and examines everything from menstruation to the global politics of women's health. Another book that is not only informative but engaging is *Growing Up: It's a Girl Thing* by Mavis Jukes. This book is written for adolescent girls, but it is so humorous that parents will find themselves reading it as well.

After parents and daughters have mastered the anatomical changes, they need to become familiar with the spiritual ones as well. The most obvious spiritual transformation that occurs as a result of a girl's first moon cycle involves a shift in her divine essence. This shift is caused by a material awareness of sorts that occurs as the elements of spirit and water meet with earth. Before she docks at the outer world, the journeying girl lives and breathes her intuition. She is pure spirit (her inner world) and water (emotion). Her actions are based on her simplistic, psychical nature. Basically, she pretty much calls things as she sees them. However, once her barge merges with solid earth (the adult world) her perception expands to include the dense, multidimensional, material world. As she gazes upon this outer world, she finds that her thoughts are no longer fueled purely by her spirit. In fact, it is just the opposite—her spirit becomes ignited and engaged only through her conscious thoughts.

This abrupt awareness can be related to the moment that Eve pulled that first juicy apple off the Tree of Life and bit into it. The adolescent girl suddenly equates her unbridled intuition with being naked. She feels exposed at having nothing but her own insights with which to clothe herself, and so she seeks to cover her spirit up with the material world. Like mixing flour and water to make a paste, she takes the fluid, inner-nature of her own being, and literally infuses it with the earth of the outer world. The moment she does this, she becomes divine potential manifested in a solid form. She is no longer simply spirit, she is substance. She is clay on the potter's wheel, ready to be molded and formed by her own hands into a masterpiece.

It is a painful process, though—this kneading of the elements. Any time two worlds collide there is a certain amount of discomfort. For a few months the mixing of the outer world and the inner world leaves both worlds deluded and transposed. During this time of mixing, the journeying girl is left with a feeling of being misplaced. This feeling of being lost and misplaced is different than when the pre-adolescent girl was floating between the two worlds. Now she is taking who she is spiritually and actually blending it with the adult world. Although the adolescent girl is excited to have her first period, her new essence leaves her feeling spiritually alienated from both worlds. It is as though she is no longer spirit, and no longer physical. She is a new entity that is both. She will exist as this new spiritual/physical self for the next several decades, until once again the two are separated as she journeys back into the inner world during menopause. In the meantime, she must become accustomed to it, this settling of spirit and body. If she is wise, she will learn to use this uncomfortable feeling to her advantage in navigating her way through the adult world. And hopefully, she will hold the remembrance of what it was like when she lived completely in the inner world.

Emotionally, an adolescent girl feels that now that she has started her moon cycle she is an adult. She no longer wants to just look like an adult, she wants to be treated like an adult. For in her mind, she is an adult. Unfortunately, or fortunately, however the case may be, this is simply not true. Just because an adolescent girl's body has enough estrogen in it to produce a period every month, doesn't mean that she is wise enough to make adult decisions. And it will probably take several years and quite a few mistakes before a journeying girl understands this concept. Until then, she will continue to push the limits set by her parents. And as she moves into the fifth ritual, this need to push the limits with her parents will become even more complicated as she steps off of the barge and enters the world of men.

"The effect of living backwards,"
the Queen said kindly:
"it always makes one a
little giddy at first."

THE FIFTH RITE

Living on the Banks of the Outer World

AS AN ADOLESCENT GIRL'S excitement builds, she reaches a point where she can no longer be a spectator—she simply must be an active participant in the adult world. And so, having completed her first menstrual cycle, she steps off her barge and onto the soft, squishy, sand-like shores of the outer world. Because she has been voyaging on the turbulent waters of puberty for quite some time, her first movements are awkward and clumsy. She is like a new calf learning to walk on legs that are much too long and flimsy. Nevertheless, upon gaining her footing in the new land, she intently scrambles away from the water and her barge without so much as a single look back. To the journeying girl, the party of adolescence has just begun.

The scenery on the outer shore is almost too breathtaking for words. It is a virtual wonderland of imagery. There are myriad things to see and do. There are dances and cosmetics and friends. There are boys and dating and first kisses. And most of all there is a sense of freedom and independence of which the adolescent girl has never experienced. She is physically free from her parents' watchful eye, she is emotionally free from the drifting barge, and she is spiritually free from her own inner voice which she haphazardly suppressed the moment she stepped foot on dry land. However, these bright, animated beaches of the adult world are truly a distortion of what the interior land is like. In fact, the beach is a mirage to what really lies ahead. As time passes, and as a girl moves closer to the center of the adult world, the sights will dull and the land will become rigid and barren in many places. But for the next few years, at least, she will find the new ground flexible and the view absolutely dazzling.

The adolescent girl is ecstatic to be ashore and finds herself overwhelmed with giddiness as she trots along the beach. She becomes quite paradoxical and inconsistent at this point in her journey. She is practically intoxicated by the sights and sounds of the outer world, and her newfound freedom has her head spinning in all directions. In fact, this giddiness, which may appear in the form of irresponsible, illogical and frivolous behavior, is one of the hallmarks of this fifth rite. Unfortunately, the explosive combination with the other hallmark, which is her developing relationship with the opposite sex, doesn't seem to make this fifth ritual flow any smoother.

Now that the girl is in the outer world, which is under the jurisdiction of men, she must conform to a new set of rules. She must make a place for herself in a world where prizes are doled out to the most testosterone driven, and thus her intuition is practically worthless. This is not an easy task for a being whose body is being infused with estrogen and whose most treasured skill, up until this point, has been her sixth sense. To further complicate matters, her relationship with the opposite sex takes on a multidimensional nature as she moves further inland. Not only has the adolescent girl evolved during her voyage across the water, but adolescent boys have made their own journey and have grown as well.

The maturation of adolescent boys, as well as that of adolescent girls, forces an obvious shift in the way the two genders communicate as they reconnect on the outer shores. Raging hormones and sexual tension suddenly come into play, intensifying emotions for both sexes. This produces a more in-depth quality to the female/male exchange, and conversations between the two take on intricate, maze-like tones. The world of boys suddenly seems very complex to the adolescent girl. This complexity brings about a fascination with these mysterious male creatures, which only serves to deepen her desire for their approval. Furthermore, finding herself on unfamiliar ground, she begins to slip and fall in many places. The rules of interaction have reversed, and her self-esteem, having taken quite a beating in the barge, is still bruised. In an effort to be friendly with the natives and find some stability, her charitable nature takes over. She is eager to please and is willing to go to great lengths to ingratiate herself into the male culture.

In fact, this fifth ritual marks the time when many an adolescent girl hands over her soulskin. It is at this point, when she is on the outer shores of this new, exciting land, that the relinquishment of her spirit seems like a small price to pay for admission. She is eager to accommodate the inhabitants of the outer world, and they too are eager to take what she has to offer. If the adolescent girl has a strong spirit and has been properly prepared, she will know the value of her pelt and her soul. And she will understand that those who are worthy of her love will welcome her without asking her to pay such a high price. However, if she is not careful, her altruistic nature can trip her up even more, and her misguided efforts to gain footing will instead land her back in the water without a barge or a soulskin.

Over time, and through trial and error, most girls eventually master the relationship ropes by slowly integrating themselves into the outer world, while at the same time integrating men into theirs. Sooner or later they learn, as all wise-women do, that merely standing with a man on the ground of his world will not bring about a true intimacy. They will come to recognize that standing with a man, while at the same time transporting him into the sacred recesses of their own inner world, will produce a much deeper connection. They also eventually learn that the ability to create successful relationships can only be mastered if they hang onto their soulskin, and only if they are spiritually mature enough to fasten a place for themselves in both worlds.

The inner circle is the ethereal space that exists around all creatures. It is much like an energy field in that it either attracts or repels. The inner circle of a girl's being is where she attracts or repels good into her life. It also represents the place where she interacts with close friends and family, and it is within this dimension that she is most likely to share her emotions and feelings. Unlike the soulskin, which can be taken or given away at will, the inner circle is permanent. It is the constant, steadfast realm that reflects the true nature of her soul. But again, it is not her soul, and there is a big difference between allowing another person to penetrate one's inner circle and allowing them to penetrate one's soul. To merge with another soul is a very momentous act; it is something that should be reserved for only a few. And although it is certainly important to be discrete about sharing space in one's inner circle, it does not carry the same grave consequences that sharing one's soul does.

The unofficial welcoming of priests (males) to her inner circle is probably the safest way in which a girl can connect with the opposite sex. It is a way in which she can share what it means to be born female and at the same time get an understanding of what it means to be born male without formally committing her soul. In many ways it allows her to get her feet wet while still keeping her head above the male-female relationship waters. And most importantly, it is a way in which she can share a piece of her heart with the boys in her life without giving away her soulskin.

This ritualistic welcoming of priests to the inner circle of a girl's being commences the moment she is born. As a maiden, the dance had a slow, familiar rhythm to it. A young girl's experiences with the male populace were nearly always from the point of view of her sacred, inner world, and were limited to alliances with family members and young play-mates. Ideally, these relationships were virtuous and simplistic. Communication between the genders was sincere, direct and effortless. All and all, these positive qualities, mixed with the girl's own self-confidence, usually made for pretty healthy relationships. In fact, these alliances, especially the one with her father, becomes the foundation on which a young girl builds her adult relationships with men in the outer world.

Psychologists have long been aware of the emotional role that a father plays in his daughter's life. Statistics show that adolescent girls who get the least amount of attention and approval from their fathers at home are the most likely to seek inappropriate sexual attention from boys at school. And yet statistics also show that the time around puberty, in which an adolescent girl is most in need of her father's admiration, is also the time in which fathers begin to pull away. For not only is the girl changing, but her father is changing emotionally as well. Little girls suddenly become women, the opposite sex, and the whole father/daughter dance takes on a new perspective. Even fathers who have previously had very close, loving relationships with their daughters tend to recoil. Why the about-face? And why now, when a girl is most in need of her father, does he retreat?

This decrease in the display of affection and closeness that a man shows his daughter at this point in the journey is often the result of his uneasiness with her budding sexuality. Many men find it difficult to relate to their daughters once their bodies start to mature. Adolescent girls, suddenly aware of their own sexuality, are also, for the first time, starting to react to daddy's discomfort. They are perplexed by the odd way in which their fathers have begun to respond to their womanhood, and so they begin to close the relationship door, or at least guard it a little more carefully. They sense their father's resistance, and they themselves begin to resist. Suddenly, these male figures become more than just a parent; they, too, are seen primarily as the opposite sex. At this point, the welcoming of fathers to the inner circle can become very complicated indeed. But it doesn't have to be that way.

In fact, this time in a girl's journey can be a very special time for bonding and getting reacquainted. It was during this stage, when I was entering my own fifth ritual of menarche, that my parents divorced. Up until this time I was not especially close with my father, but I found this sudden separation from him very unsettling. So much so that I ended up electing to live with him during my last years of high school. We grew very close during these years and he taught me many things about men that I don't think I would have ever learned if I had remained in my mother's house. To this day, I feel that we have a certain understanding about each other's lives that no one else shares.

However, a father and daughter don't have to remain under the same roof in order to be close. Neither do they need to be in close physical proximity in order to share a special bond. I believe that all they really need is mutual love and respect. This, along with a willingness on the part of both parties to accept the changes that are occurring in the relationship, will strengthen the ties and make for a lasting and healthy relationship.

It is also helpful if both father and daughter understand that their feelings of apprehension about their evolving relationship are not only normal, but are essential. These feelings become the catalyst that switch the tune from a monotonous jingle to a deep, well-orchestrated symphony. This shift in melodies is part of the normal process if the father/daughter dance is to last for any length of time. Like all relationships, in order to deepen and grow, the father/daughter rhythm must move forward. But this progression doesn't have to mean the end to the dance. The partners must simply modify a few steps to accommodate the new song.

Learning a new parental dance just when he feels he's got the old one down is not an easy task for any father. In fact, in the beginning, it can feel like walking a tightrope. But a new pattern of relating can eventually be established with a lot of patience and a lot of faith. Instead of giving into his uneasiness and withdrawing his affections, a father can take the lead and keep his valued place in the inner circle by redirecting his feelings and actions in a way that accommodate his daughter's physical changes. There will be times when he may feel like an intruder, especially on matters like menstruation, but he must push on, remembering that no matter what his daughter says or how she acts, she needs him now more than ever.

One very important step a father can make in redirecting the dance is to acknowledge his unresolved feelings about his daughter's sexuality. It is imperative for him to understand that his feelings of apprehension and confusion are not unusual. Down through time, it is something that every father has wrestled with. He must force himself to acknowledge his daughter as a sexual being, and understand that she has a right to express that sexuality without being judged. This last point is especially important, because in order for a girl to be comfortable with her sexuality, she must feel as though those around her, especially the men in her life, are comfortable with it as well.

Another step a father should make is to redirect his displays of affection to accommodate his daughter's physical maturity. For example, instead of having her sit on his lap, he can encourage her to snuggle close to his side. Instead of enfolding her into his arms during an embrace, he can make it a point to give her several short hugs throughout the day.

At the same time that he is rearranging his dance, he must continue the steady beat of praise. I don't believe that at this point in the journey a father can overstate his daughter's accomplishments. As long as the compliments on her appearance are balanced with admiration for her academic and athletic skills, and as long as the praise is sincere, then it's never too much of a good thing. Despite their egotistical nature, adolescent girls can never really be too confident, for below that concrete exterior lies a spirit that needs to be constantly reminded of its worth. And while a mother is certainly an intricate part of the scenery, it is a girl's father who is the key player in the confidence game. Being the major player in his daughter's life takes a lot of time and a lot of extra effort on his part, but it is a necessary step if the journeying girl is going to make it to the core of the adult world in one piece.

At the same time that a father is learning how to rearrange and strengthen the bond with his daughter, he must also learn how to loosen some of the ties that he has to her. Although it is important that the overall connection to her be kept, a daughter's need for privacy must also be respected. It is a difficult balance to keep. But in the end the payoff will be great, for to remain in the inner circle of his daughter's world is perhaps the greatest reward that can be bestowed on any father.

The welcoming of priests to the inner circle may begin with fathers, but it doesn't end there. The welcoming of priests into a girl's innermost recesses is a lifelong ritual that includes men of all ages and associations. It is a sacrament that can be observed with great dignity as the interchange of feelings and emotions flow between a young girl and her male companions. Unfortunately, this ritual can also be maligned if girls themselves do not first acknowledge and recognize the value of their own gifts. Their views on how they perceive themselves, and what they have to offer the world, influences the way in which they allow men into their lives.

The passageway into a girl's heart is always through her spirit, and visa versa; in many ways, the two are intertwined. Rarely does a girl give her heart to a boy, that her spirit doesn't find a way to tag along. And likewise, when a girl offers the gift of her spirit up to a companion, her heart is usually packed neatly inside. The trouble is, at this point in the journey, the adolescent girl's heart is quite unstable, and her intuitive spirit has pretty much taken a back seat to the male population in general. Fortunately, there is a built-in gate at the opening of every girl's inner circle that acts as a sort of check point. In order for a male to gain access to the sacred inner circle of a girl's being, he must past through this ethereal gate or opening. It is a very versatile opening, this gate. Although it is formed through the experiences she has with her father and with other prominent males in her life, the opening and closing of the gate can be altered at her discretion.

There are three basic ways in which an adolescent girl operates the gate to her inner circle. Unfortunately, the two most widely used methods are also the most detrimental to her self-esteem and self-worth. One of these occurs when a girl opens the gate so wide that every male in the general vicinity wanders in. This expansion at the entrance to her heart usually occurs when a girl is desperate for male companionship. Many times the adolescent girl, through a very tragic relationship with her father, or other male in her life, is left with a very low opinion of her gifts. This low self-esteem eats a colossal hole through what should be a very protective covering to her inner gateway. Over the years this already gaping hole stretches with every painful experience in which males are involved. Pretty soon, there is no inner circle at all—there is only the depleted adolescent girl who no longer can distinguish between healthy and unhealthy relationships.

Alternatively, this vast widening of the gate can also come about as the result of a young girl never having experienced any male/female relationship, healthy or otherwise. At the time of adolescence, in a desperate and misguided attempt to grab the attention of any man, she will throw open her gate to every guy who comes along. This enormous hole in the inner circle of an adolescent girl's heart is truly a tragic thing. Often she becomes a victim in very abusive relationships.

The other mistake an adolescent girl makes in tending the gate to her inner circle is to keep all men out. Many times adolescent girls, in an effort to safeguard their inner world, never allow any male—friend or lover—to penetrate the circle. Although this may seem like a wiser choice than letting every male inside, in reality, it is equally as unhealthy. To never experience the joy of sharing one's inner circle with the opposite sex, even in a platonic relationship, is heartbreaking. Like the girl who opened her gate for every man, this over-guarding of the passageway to her inner sphere usually stems from being uncomfortable around males because there were no men in her life, or because the men in her life were so unbearable that she prefers not to have any type of relationship with the opposite sex at all. Although the consequences of this scenario are not quite as obvious as when an adolescent girl allows every man inside, it is still a lonely and depressing existence. When the inner circle is closed so tightly that no man can enter, the girl becomes an emotional and spiritual hermit. She misses out on the multitude of wondrous and magical gifts that only the male gender can bring into her life.

The third, and optimally best approach for a journeying girl to take when allowing men into her inner circle, is to engage a screening process. This screening process is an intellectual sifter of sorts that allows a girl to separate the healthy relationships from the unhealthy ones. It is also an emotional net that immediately snags and prohibits any maligned companions from raiding her inner world. If an adolescent girl is able to filter out the males who are not in tune with her highest good, then she will be able to bypass many unnecessary heartaches on her journey to womanhood. She will also be able to experience male/female friendships in the way that was intended by the creator. And if this net is built with the best of intentions, then it will help her find a mate who is not only compatible physically and emotionally, but who will nurture her spiritually as well.

In order to set up a screening process, an adolescent girl must be clear on what is healthy versus unhealthy behavior in a relationship. She must be able to differentiate between high risk behavior and behavior that is nurturing and a conduit to her own needs. Unfortunately, at this stage in the journey, most girls don't know the difference. And while they can certainly weed out boys who are obviously plagued, there are many red flag behaviors that even grown women fall victim to. The obvious atrocities, such as emotional and physical violence, can be pointed out by parents. The not so obvious transgressions such as manipulation, incompatibility and dishonesty are behaviors that a young girl will have to discern for herself.

This delicate part of the netting is something that she will have to fashion alone. It is something that takes time, and unfortunately, is often learned only through trial and error. However, by remembering to use her intuition, she can, over time, build herself a strong and sturdy sieve that will allow her to receive openly and honestly the valuable gifts of men who are true, while at the same time refusing to participate in nonproductive relationships with men who are not. It is also important that a journeying girl establish these standards for friends who are boys as well as for boyfriends.

Of course, no screening process is perfect, and it is inevitable that over the years every girl will find herself in at least one unhealthy relationship. If she is aware of her worth and her power, and where her power originates, then this ominous relationship will be short-lived. She will learn how to cut her losses early, and move on quickly. If not, parents may have to intercede.

One of the most vivid memories I have of my teenage years is of my mother spread eagle against our front door. I had announced that I was going to go out with an older boy and was attempting to leave the house. This boy, who had already been expelled from school on numerous occasions, had parked in front, and was honking the horn. As I tried to leave, my mother, who is petite and who, even when I was fifteen, was much shorter than I, plastered herself against the front door and emphatically stated, "Over my dead body!" Despite my screams and threats, my mother never budged. And as much as I wanted to be with this boy, I knew that I probably would have to kill her in order to get by, so I eventually backed down. Although I don't recommend this type of strong-arm approach in most parent-daughter conflicts, I do believe that on occasions such as this, parents need to take a firm stand, as this type of militant action is often the only way to keep a headstrong teenage girl safe.

That doesn't mean, however, that adolescent boys are always the cause of unhealthy relationships.

Many times it is the actions of the adolescent girl that plague the male/female dance. One of the most widespread abuses of feminine power by young girls, and indeed by women, is the flaunting of their sexuality. It is odd that, despite the feminism of the sixties and the increased opportunities that are given women as we move into the twenty-first century, sex (and the presumed sexual power that women have over men) still plays such a significant role in the male/female dance. But it does.

While society has pretty much abandoned the belief that women can get anything they want through sexual favors, there is still a lot of emphasis put on a woman's ability to get what she needs by virture of her sexuality. It is the last remaining power play left in an unwritten, archaic dating manual. It is an unspoken rule, that, like the proverbial ace up the sleeve, a girl can count on her sexuality to elevate her standing in her relationships with boys. It is also the one-upmanship she has over other girls who are less desirable. And no matter how well we immerse our daughters in the dogma of intellectual attraction, it is the inherent value of their sexuality that they play to the hilt during this fifth ritual. Therefore, the question isn't how do we keep them from misusing their sexuality in a relationship, but how do we help them view their sexuality in the proper perspective? How do we teach them to balance their sexuality with other desirable attributes such as intelligence, spirituality and emotional stability?

I believe that the most effective way to offset an adolescent girl's tendency to rely on her sexuality rather than her intellect is by example. This may seem like a simple solution to a very complex problem. But there is truly no better way to get the point across. Surrounding a girl with women who have made their mark by flexing their intellectual muscles drives the point home, and it does it in a way that is neither heavy-handed nor obvious. And getting this point across is imperative if girls are going to make their way into the core of the adult world in one piece. They need to know that their sexuality is certainly a vital part of who they are, but they also need to understand that it is something to be shared out of a desire to be intimate, not out of the desire to get ahead.

As a journeying girl continues her attempts to physically connect with the male gender, she will also make attempts to spiritually and emotionally communicate with them. Because she is often more emotionally mature than her male counterpart, she will find that her attempts to relate her feelings are thwarted early on. She will, of course, continue to try to make an emotional connection with males throughout her life, but for now she will most likely turn her attentions to making a soul connection with them. For although she stands on the ground of the outer world, she still carries the weapons and skills of her inner world. And at some point during this ritual, she will pull out and dust off her spiritual arsenal as a means of connecting.

One of the many ways an adolescent girl will attempt to spiritually connect with boys is through her dreams. The association of dreams with spirit has been around since recorded history, and is found in nearly all sacred writings. This correlation comes out of the need to bring meaning, most notably a divine meaning, to our dreams. In fact, this need to bring meaning to our dreams is so strong that we often interpret our dreams to be prophecies of our waking life. Whether they are mirror images of our waking life, or whether our waking life is truly a reflection of our dreams, remains to be seen. One thing is for certain, though, and that is that our dreams bring to life the objects of our desire in a way that could never happen when we are awake. By connecting with someone in our dreams, we are connecting in a nonphysical manner. We are touching what we are unable to touch in our waking lives. And for the hormone-infused adolescent girl, these unreachable, untouchable objects happen to be boys.

In their dreams, adolescent girls are able to act out at night what they wouldn't be caught dead doing during the day. At this point in the journey, these dreams usually involve kissing and other light physical touch, as light physical touch is truly all that journeying girls are seeking at this point. They're merely wanting the spiritual and emotional connection to be made. They are not seeking to physically merge, as boys their age are seeking to do with them. Again, they are simply wanting to connect, and through dreams they are able to accomplish this.

The increase in estrogen also has its effects, not only on a girl's libido, but on her dream recall. Surges of estrogen often produces a deeper sleep, and the REM (deepest part of sleep) period also seems to be longer. Many parents are often dismayed to find out that their daughter is sleep-walking occasionally. These deep periods of sleep will come during the time when a girl's estrogen is peaking, normally halfway through her menstrual cycle, and should subside as her body adjusts to the higher hormone levels.

As the adolescent girl continues to connect with boys on several different levels, she will find herself moving away from the beaches of the outer world and onto the firmer, more stable soil. She will find that her responsibilities increase as she moves inland and she will find that, as these responsibilities increase, her intuitive nature begins to fade.

Physically, spiritually, emotionally and mentally these first years on the shores of the outer world have been tough. But the changes she made here are some of the most important ones she will ever make. Hopefully, she will have laid a strong foundation for the coming rituals. For as she journeys into the next rite, in which she will leave the soft beaches and move deeper into the interior of the outer world, she will need this strong foundation in order to survive.

"I SHOULD see the garden far better,"
said Alice to herself, "if I could get
to the top of that hill: and here's a
path that leads straight to it . . . .
But how curiously it twists! It's
more like a corkscrew than a path!"

THE SIXTH RITE
Moving Inland

AFTER SEVERAL YEARS of socializing on the outer
shore, a journeying girl's spirit once again begins to
stir, and a prophetic call, much like the one she
heard during her preadolescent days, beckons to her
from deep within the core of the outer world. She
has grown weary of the superficial relationships she
has formed on the shores, and wants to bring a more
profound meaning to her life. She intuitively knows
that by leaving the shallow beaches and travelling
deeper into the outer world she will find the purpose
that she seeks. But the roads that lead to the core of
the adult world are shaded and undefined, while the
beach is carefree and light. And she isn't quite sure

of what will be expected of her once she leaves the outer shores, so she thinks long and hard about continuing her journey. And indeed she should. This spiritual decision to pack up her psyche and move inland takes more time and consideration than any other one she has had to make. It is not one that can be rushed. And it is not one that a parent or friend can make for her.

The decision to move inland can only be made after a teenage girl understands on a deep down, soul level, that *being* a woman is more than just *looking* like one. Up until now, in her mind at least, dressing like a woman, having a menstrual cycle like a woman, and dating like a woman meant that she was a woman. And on the soft beaches of the outer world, she was indeed a woman. But there is a big difference between being an adult on the banks, or surface, of the outer world, and truly being an adult in the core. And this is the lesson that the teenage girl learns during this sixth ritual.

The official beginning of this rite commences the moment the journeying girl awakens to the fact that she will truly be an adult only after she has ventured beyond the fringes and been initiated into the core of the outer world as childbearer. Comprehending this truth is not easy, though. In fact, it often takes a lot of forethought on the part of the teenage girl to formally abandon the beaches. In order to do this she must be willing to temporarily leave many of the pleasures behind and travel some pretty treacherous roads. And she must do so on the wings of her own power and strength. Like the voyage across the waters, the journey inland is not one which supports hitchhikers or stowaways. That is why the final decision to leave the beaches must be hers and hers alone.

More often than not, awakening to what it truly means to be an adult comes only after a teenage girl has learned to distinguish between simple pleasure and true gratification. The journeying girl usually learns the difference between the two only after a certain amount of self-indulgence. Pleasure, she discovers, is short-lived, and gratification, which involves satisfying the needs of another person, is long-lasting. But there are few chances to find gratification on the outer shores and so she finds herself spending most of her time feeling lonely and incomplete. These feelings prompt her to further investigate her surroundings and the opportunities the shore provides her. And more importantly, they lead her to examine her own spirit. What she finds in her environment as well as in her soul is not always comfortable. In fact, like most awakenings, it is often quite painful.

The first thing a girl notices as she begins to awaken is that although the scenery is beautiful, the topography is flat. There are no mountains and no valleys on the sand. In fact, the beach seems almost spiritless. Furthermore, there is a lack of commitment among the occupants. The young women and men here have limited obligations and ties. In general, life on the shore become less and less enchanting to the journeying girl as she begins to truly comprehend the adage that all that glitters is not gold. Eventually a light bulb goes off, and she is able to clearly see that there is more to the outer world than satisfying her own desires.

Understanding that there is more to life than her own pleasure is a true spiritual revelation. Up until this point, the teenage girl's journey has been driven by a superficial longing to experience the titillating comforts of the adult world. Tempted by the calling of these pleasures, she left her inner island, travelled over the emotional waters and abandoned her barge for life on the sandy shore. And for quite some time the sampling of these adult treats satisfied her. To the adolescent girl, looking like an adult was the same as being an adult and so, in her eyes, these sensual trappings were all there was to the outer world. But now the difference between pleasure (the beach) and gratification (the core) becomes more than just obvious. It becomes overwhelming.

Suddenly, the teenage girl is not only no longer interested in the pleasures of the outer banks, she is repelled by them. She yearns for spiritual strength and depth—something she knows that she will never find there. She realizes that in order to find this strength and depth, and truly be an adult, she must be willing to take on more responsibility and obligations. She also intuitively knows that she must also be willing to give as well as receive. It is at this point, as she stands on the imaginary border that separates the outer shores from the roads inland and contemplates this new awareness, that the rigid, shadowy paths seem inconsequential. She has no choice but to leave the beaches and forge ahead.

The age at which a girl moves through this sixth ritual varies more than any of the other rites. Girls typically begin to inch away from the banks somewhere between their 15th and 16th birthday, but they may leave as early as 14 or as late as 19. This variance in age is dependent on many factors, the most obvious one being emotional maturity. A young woman must have a fair amount of control over her emotions to survive the journey inland. She must be able to reign in her passions when needed, and be able to direct her energies in a disciplined manner. She must also be able to exercise good, old fashion common sense in order to navigate the road ahead, for once she leaves, she leaves for good.

This is not to say that she cannot take short trips back now and then. In fact, taking a few jaunts back to the beach is not only permitted, but it is necessary if she is to last for any length of time in the nucleus of the outer world. However, she must understand that once she leaves the coastline, she makes an unspoken commitment to spending her days tending to the responsibilities that come with being a true childbearer.

Unfortunately, some girls never realize this. They either attempt to keep one foot firmly planted in each place, or they spend all their time streaking up and down the roads trying to get from the beach to the core and back before anyone misses them in either spot. In essence, trying to live on the coast and in the core of the outer world is like trying to live two lives simultaneously. And what will usually happen if a girl attempts to do this is that she will not only run herself ragged, but she will never find any sort of peace on either ground.

Another hurdle at the beginning of this sixth ritual occurs when girls decide never to leave the shores at all. They stay on the fringes of life, never really experiencing any kind of depth. They are the women who mix growing up with growing old, and hence bury themselves in the sandy shores playing beach blanket bingo way past sundown. They do this not only because they fear growing old, but also because they fear true intimacy. But as every wise-woman knows, genuine communion between two souls never occurs on the sandy beaches of life. By its very nature, intimacy is centralized. It is intense and intestinal. It is deep-seated and enclosed. And it is something that cannot be found skirting around the banks of the outer world. Many times the women who waste their time and their lives trying to spiritually connect on the fringes of life are the same ones who, during the fifth ritual, either locked the gate to their inner circle or have had it swinging open for so long that all available companions have moved inland without them. And just as was discussed during the fifth ritual, the confusion between spiritual intimacy and sexual intimacy is what keeps them thinking they've found the real thing when all they've really found is someone with whom to pass the time.

Again, true intimacy occurs when a girl willfully takes that first step off the powdery beaches and onto the rough terrain of her life. It is her formal declaration to grow up and to grow on. This first step marks her intentions to move into what is informally called her childbearing years. Of course, just because a girl has decided to move inland, doesn't mean that she will take on the responsibility of motherhood. Before a woman is ready to bear a child, she must have a certain amount of experience bearing the world. And this is something that takes many years of living in the core to accomplish. When a teenage girl leaves the beach and migrates toward the core to become a childbearer, it is simply her announcement to the world that she is aware that there is more to the adult world than just the self-absorbed outer shores.

If parents find that their daughter seems to be having a hard time leaving the beaches, they can try to gently coax her off. However, they should never try to force her into making that decision. Authoritative parenting only serves to make a teenage girl more determined to dig her heels into the sand. One of the best ways to get a girl started on the path to responsibility is by providing her with a positive role model. This role model should be a woman who knows how to share her gifts without giving away her power. A mother or other relative who spends an appropriate amount of time volunteering is a perfect example. In fact, becoming a volunteer is a gentle and yet persistent way to allow an adolescent girl to become acquainted with the responsibilities of the adult world. It permits her to venture down the path a short distance without obligating her to the role of childbearer just yet. It also allows her to explore any future job interests she may have. But in the end, parents must remember that while it is okay to gently coax their daughter off the beaches, it is better in the long run for everyone involved if she leaves by her own accord. Truly, the decision to leave the beaches and start on the path toward her childbearing years should come from within her soul.

A teenage girl's resolution to leave the edges of the outer world is a major proclamation in her life. It indicates that she is ready to take on the obligations that come with being a childbearer. The responsibility of childbearing means more than just bearing children, though. In many ways it means that she will be bearing, or sustaining the world. And truly, that is what a woman does when she gives life, whether it is done through nurturing a child of her own, or by nurturing mankind as a whole. For to give a life is the same as to give *of* one's life. It means offering one's gifts unconditionally, and being of service (which should not be confused with being subservient). During the journey of menarche, it is transitioning from a girl who acts in accordance with her own good, to a woman who acts in accordance with the good of everyone.

Becoming a true childbearer also means being of use while at the same time not being used. In many ways it is a difficult role to master, and that is why it is so much better that the journeying girl be allowed to stay on the beach until the timekeeper of her soul signals her to leave. Girls who leave the shores prematurely or are forced to take on the responsibilities of the world before their souls are truly ready are often doomed to getting lost on the path.

As time passes, the desire to move deeper into the outer world almost becomes an obsession, until finally she gives into the feeling and turns away from the animated shores. The next decision she must make is which of the two roads to take—the long one or the short one. All in all, it doesn't matter which one she chooses: Both roads lead to the same place—accountability. And as every parent knows, accountability, which is truly what being an adult means, is something that can only be learned by receiving some hard knocks along the way. Fortunately, or unfortunately, depending on how you look at it, both roads provide the teenage girl with enough opportunities to learn this lesson.

Of course, to most neophytes, the shorter road often appears to be the best one to take because of the time factor. And for the teenage girl, who is often very shortsighted in her thinking, this becomes her first choice. What she doesn't anticipate, though, is how scary and intimidating the obscureness of the shortcut is. In essence, this road is the condensed version of the longer road, without the breathing room. It is fast-paced, and virtually littered with potholes and scary creatures. Temptations and mirages seem to appear from out of nowhere. I can't help but think of Alice in *Through the Looking-Glass* as she moves along the checkered countryside in search of the "eight square," dodging strange creatures and insects.

Luckily, the journeying girl, like Alice, takes some inner world companions along to help her. Like the Red Queen, who represents brain-power, she has her intellect to provide a wise council in helping her bypass the temptations. These temptations that line the road to the inner core are really just decoys and misguided directions. They are, in essence, the dead end streets and blind alleys that tend to lead the girl in circles. And on this compressed road to accountability there are many of these detours. Some of the temptations, such as sex, can be handled by relying on her inner guide. Some temptations, such as drugs, should never be handled at all. However, if she exercises her brain-power and pays attention to the warning signs which come in the form of plain old common sense, she will find herself dashing past both of them with little time wasted.

Another companion that comes into play and can be of great assistance on this short, dangerous road, is the keeper of her heart. Like the clumsy but brave White Knight, who represented Alice's heart, the keeper of the journeying girl's heart helps her keep a lid on her emotions. It is similar to the net at the entrance of her inner world, which she fashioned in the last ritual, in that it helps her distinguish between good and evil. It is the litmus test that she uses to verify what is true and what is not. And it is what keeps her faithful to her mission, which is to reach adulthood in one piece. With these two helpers and her own brave spirit, the journeying girl will eventually make it through the forest over the river and into the core of the outer world.

The alternate road to accountability is the longer, lucid, more even trail. This path comes through many years of easy but steadfast travelling. It utilizes the "put one foot in front of the other and keep moving" method, and it is the easiest path to take in the long run. Although it takes more time to move through puberty and into adulthood, in the end, a girl is more likely to arrive at the core in one piece. Unfortunately, few girls have the maturity at the onset of their journey to choose this path. By their very nature, teenage girls are shortsighted and impatient. They also tend to be a little overconfident when it comes to their ability to fend off dangers. But, again, which road they choose to take is a decision that only they can make. Like the timing of their journey, it is controlled by their own internal instruments and persona.

During this sixth ritual, and the next one, the journeying girl will toughen up emotionally. The hardening of her emotions comes as a result of leaving the soft flexible beaches and traversing through the slippery and uneven path to the core of the outer world. The many bumps and bruises that she will get along the way will become the battle scars that will elevate her perception of those around her. Along the road she will also learn to distinguish between those who truly need her help and those indolent souls who only want to ride her coattails. She will learn, too, that emotion is a powerful weapon that, when used proficiently and precisely, can quicken her senses and keep her out of harm's way.

The transitioning girl will not change as much physically as she has in the past rituals. By now her adult height has been reached and any alterations in her appearance will come in the form of weight gain as her figure continues to fill out. Although it is quite normal, the gaining of even a few pounds at this time is often a major concern for teenage girls, and again parents need to be vigilant about eating disorders. However, the vigilance should not be placed on the food, but rather on how the girl feels about herself. For as most doctors who deal with eating disorders will confirm, the disorder is not about food at all. It is about control and self-esteem.

Hormonally speaking, the teenage girl is experiencing regular moon cycles, and her estrogen levels are peaking. In addition to estrogen and progesterone, she is also starting to make a significant amount of testosterone. Testosterone, which is normally thought of only as a male hormone, is also important to the well-being of a woman. It is what keeps her active and strong, and it is what governs her libido. What started in the fifth rite as a sexual awakening shifts into overdrive during this sixth ritual. And just because she has left the beach and is moving inland to a life of more responsibility, doesn't mean she has abandoned her sexuality. In fact, because of the increase in testosterone, sex often takes center stage on the roads inland. Only now, the consequences of acting out her sensual nature in unhealthy ways becomes more dangerous than ever.

Along the road her passions will run high and the romantic dreams of the last ritual become more sexually oriented in this one. Furthermore, not only will she be fantasizing about boys, but she will be acting these fantasies out. Statistics from The National Campaign to Prevent Pregnancy show that one of every three girls has had sex by age sixteen, and two out of three by age eighteen. And despite warnings from parents and teachers, they are doing so without the proper protection. In their book, *All That She Can Be*, Dr. Carol J. Eagle and Carol Comanstate state that one third of all teenage girls do not use contraception the first time that they have intercourse. Furthermore, according to the Center for Disease Control and Prevention the highest rates of gonorrhea and chlamydia in women are found in 15- to 19-year-olds. Needless to say, the dangers of a girl becoming pregnant or contacting a sexually transmitted disease is very real at this point in the journey, and parents should be aware that even with the proper preparation from them, the hormone-saturated detours of puberty are often too much for a girl to resist.

In addition to navigating around their sexual feelings, teenage girls also become very distracted by the social scene. Although the very act of leaving the beaches behind shows a certain amount of self-confidence on their part, they still lack the courage to totally defy peer pressure. High school itself brings a whole new set of problems. This is often a painful time for girls as well as for boys, and it is important for both genders to be aware that they are not alone in their battle to climb the social ranks.

Spiritually, the teenage girl has an airtight view on religious matters and a strong desire to share them with the outside world. These fixed beliefs, though sometimes overbearing, can actually be quite helpful in her journey down the road of the sixth ritual. They will help her keep her eye on the star that lies at the core of the inner world, and they will prevent her from getting sidetracked by the temptations along the way. One of the many ways that her spirit expresses itself during this rite is through volunteer work. If she has been provided with a positive role model on how to give of her time and energy wisely, then she can become quite proficient at being a childbearer even before she reaches the inner core. Again, volunteering and being of service will expedite her journey inland and keep her from getting derailed along the way.

As the teenage girl nears the end of her pilgrimage inland, she becomes quite confident and self-assured in her ability to navigate whatever path she chooses to be on. She is, in essence, strong, self-confident, and generally feels quite good about herself. She has navigated the rough roads of puberty and is on the brink of breaking through to the core. With one hard push, she cracks open the shell, and, like a young chick who has burst through the jagged opening of the egg, thrusts her head and being into the center of the outer world.

*"Oh, how glad I am to get here! And what is this
on my head?" she exclaimed in a tone of dismay, as
she put her hands up to something very heavy, that
fitted tight round her head. "But how can it have
got there without my knowing it?" she said to herself,
as she lifted it off, and set it on her lap to make out
what it could possibly be. It was a golden crown.*

THE SEVENTH RITE
The Core of the Outer World

THE INDUCTION INTO the core of the outer world is
a major milestone in a young woman's life. It is the
culmination of all that she has journeyed for. It
marks the end of adolescence and the beginning of
her years as a full-fledged woman. It also marks the
end to the roller coaster of emotions she endured
during the last several rites. For the next two decades
she will stabilize spiritually, emotionally and
physically. She will continue to grow in all of these
areas, of course. But this growth will be more of

an expansion rather than a transition, for her movements will be confined to a centralized space as she builds on the foundation of the core. This centralized space will supply her with a safe, permanent platform in which to spread her divine wings and further hone her talents as a bearer of the world. It will also provide her with the stability that she so desperately seeks. In essence, this ritual is the one in which a young woman plants her feet on fresh soil without sinking, and, in finding that she is stable, begins to truly interact in a more balanced and mature manner.

However, just because a young woman has found her equilibrium doesn't mean that this last ritual is simplistic or effortless. In fact, the seventh ritual is, for the most part, the most complicated and intricately woven of all the rituals. Although the journey to adulthood is behind her, the young woman is still facing some major adjustments in her life, and these adaptations to the core of the outer world can be just as painful as some of the challenges she experienced during the first six rites.

In many ways this seventh rite is really four rituals in one. For over the several years it takes to acclimate herself to the core, a young woman's perception of her surroundings will shift at least four separate times. Unlike the previous rituals, in which the journeying adolescent girl had a solitary view of the world around her, this last ritual provides a young woman with multidimensional viewpoints.

Instead of seeing the outer world through the blinders of a young filly, she now sees it through the eyes of an eagle. And no matter what direction she chooses to face, her peripheral vision allows her to take in the world from the other three opposing cardinal points.

Each one of these four points of direction provides a young woman with a colorful, panoramic view. However, because she is constantly aware of what lies to the left, right and behind her, each direction also becomes a distracting force. So no matter which direction she is facing, no matter what point of view she may be holding at any particular time, there is an almost hyperawareness of the other choices. This blessing/curse is one of the great paradoxes for all young women who live in the core of the outer world. As time passes, her attention will become more focused, and although she will always be aware of the other views, her concentration will remain unchanged. But for at least the first few years in the core, the distracting viewpoints will cause a young woman to be quite whimsical in her opinions. Like the blustering winds of spring, the shifting of her beliefs can be quite unexpected and abrupt. And the manner in which the young woman views the core of the outer world is subject to change at any give time, and to change quickly.

Being aware of these sudden shifts before she reaches the core is extremely important, not only for a young woman, but for those around her as well.

Although many parents celebrate their daughter's anatomical entrance into adulthood on her 18th birthday, the exact date of her spiritual and emotional debut cannot be substantiated by time. For the most part, the spirit of an adolescent girl will make the transition into womanhood somewhere between the ages of 16 and 19. Like the official proclamation of her 18th birthday, the esoteric crossing over of the spirit into the core of the outer world is a very momentous occasion. It symbolizes a sacred union, a divine blending of energies in which her spirit marries the world and all that it represents. When a young woman moves into the core, she becomes the divine mother, caretaker and hostess to the outer world. In essence, she becomes the hand that rocks the cradle and rules the world.

As every young woman will soon find out, though, this elevated trip to the top of the pedestal comes at a price. The cheapest fare being the unofficial disappearance of her self-indulgent nature, the biggest and most costliest being the abduction of her soulskin. Still, as she stands poised on the edge of the core, the trade-off of her soulskin and ego seem like a small price to pay.

As a young woman crosses the threshold into the core of the outer world, she often feels as though she is severing the last bit of ties she had with her inner world. But this is simply not true. The solar plexus of the outer world may seem like the farthest point from the safety of her inner world because she has been journeying for so long. But it is important to remember that the farthest point from any given place is often the closest one as well, for life itself is circular and cyclical; it is a never-ending sphere of beginnings and endings and startings and stoppings. And no matter where on this infinite circle one chooses to start their journey, by the time they reach the end, they will most certainly find, if they only move far enough, that they are just inches away from where they began. So although the core of the outer world is indeed a long journey from the soft, inner recess of her spirit, it is also the most approximate. Unfortunately, this is a concept that every young woman must learn for herself. And it is a concept that she will most probably not understand until she has completed her journey through the childbearing years.

The very core of the Earth is made of iron, nickel and other minerals. And these same durable elements are what a young woman finds herself being supported by when she first steps foot in the imaginary core of the outer world. There will be many times throughout a young woman's life when she will want to use this hard surface of the core as a sort of springboard to propel her spirit back to the shores for a break, but for the most part, the steady ground will act as a foundation on which she can build her adult life.

Just how solid a young woman's foundation remains depends on many factors, the most important one being how well she navigated her journey through adolescence. Although the crystallized groundwork of the core is created by society, and those around her, her success at molding a life in this world hinges on the lessons she learned in getting there. The fashioning of her barge, her trip across the waters of puberty, her indulgent nature on the shores and the tumultuous journey on the roads inland all serve to not only mold the foundation, but to mold the woman that she becomes during this seventh rite. In essence, her ability to function and survive in the core depends on her ability to draw on her inner world, and most importantly, her ability to use what she has learned during her journey to hammer out a place for herself.

After a young woman has emotionally and spiritually settled into the core of the outer world, she begins to sense the lack of restriction that comes with living there. This freedom is what defines her second view of this new land. During the early years of this seventh ritual a young woman is overwhelmed with all that she sees. But after she has become somewhat acclimated to the rules of the road, she begins to try out her wheels, so to speak. Eventually she will begin to feel that too much is expected of her, and she will attempt to break through the hardened core. But for the present moment the young woman is so overjoyed at having finally made it to the center of the outer world that she overlooks its rigid atmosphere. She is at the front ranks. She not only looks and acts like an adult, she truly is an adult. She has responsibilities. She has obligations. And most importantly, she has the gift of freedom.

This freedom, of course, is not really a gift, but a trade-off. But from where she is standing, it not only looks like a gift, it looks like a windfall. Like her first days on the beach, she is beside herself with what to see and do first. And once again, she is literally drunk with power. She no longer wants to view. She wants to act. She has learned to drive, has a later curfew (or none at all), and is, for the most part, quite independent. This emancipation from child-hood restrictions is understandably a very gratifying time for her. She is able to play out her fantasies in ways she only dreamed about in the earlier rituals. However, while this acting out of fantasies is a dream come true for a young woman, it is a virtual nightmare for her parents.

Watching their daughter spread her wings in the core of the outer world is a scary thing for parents. In fact, it is probably the most stressful ritual for parents to endure. Not only does a young woman have the will, she has the way. The hazards of the beach and the road inland seem harmless compared to the colossal physical dangers that accompany adulthood. No longer are parents able to fix things with a band-aid. No longer are they able to guide, direct or run interference like they did in the previous rites. Consequences are beyond their control. Furthermore, during the second part of this ritual young women often have the means of getting into trouble without the sensibilities to get themselves out of it. The dangers of their daughters driving and drinking and having a run-in with the law, not to mention doing all three at the same time, becomes an ongoing nightmare for parents. What mother or father hasn't spent at least a few nights wondering where their teenage daughter was and what she was doing? And unlike the last rituals, in which parents had a certain amount of control and say so over her activities, during this ritual, the most they can do is pray for the best.

It is also important to remember, though, for peace of mind if nothing else, that most of us learned to find our way around adulthood by earning a few battle scars. Few men and women make it to adulthood without experiencing first hand the hazards of drinking too much, driving too fast, staying out too late or getting into some kind of misadventure. Yet, we survived. And if a young woman stays true to the nature of her spirit, she, too, will find the strength to navigate her early adult years in the core.

As a young woman becomes acclimated to her new-found freedom, she makes a shift into the third viewpoint. This third view is one of separation and severing of ties. She is making plans to leave her parent's house for good, and many times she often starts to disconnect from childhood friends. It is the time when she truly takes off in search of new places and new faces. It is no longer enough to have freedom, she wants distance as well. In her view, the family home is a prison, and she is the parolee. This need to disconnect is the time when young women go off to college or move into a home of their own. This physical departure mirrors a spiritual and emotional exodus as well.

The emotional and spiritual valediction that young women make can be extremely painful for parents. No matter how well planned out it was, standing at the doorway and waving farewell to their cherished child is a very difficult thing to do. Many times parents can't help but find themselves clinging to the skirt-tails of their fleeing daughter. However, if, in the hope of having a few more years of her at home, they grasp too tightly, they can incite a rebellious streak in her. That, in turn, will wreak havoc on the parent-daughter relationship, and may cause a rift that will take years to repair. In the long run, it is better if parents bravely bid adieu, even if they feel that their daughter is not ready to leave, than risk losing her all together.

Once a young woman leaves her parent's house, she finds more freedom than she ever imagined. The final severing of parental ties is exhilarating, of course, but like everything in life, this pleasure is a double-edged sword. For with the cutting of apron strings comes even more responsibilities and challenges. She must learn to cook and clean and support herself, and generally stand on her own two feet. She must contend with the rigorous life of college and/or hold down a full-time job. She has bills to pay, and exams to study for. Soon she finds that she has little, if any, time left to exercise her freedom.

Furthermore, after she has been away from home for a certain length of time, she realizes that balancing on her own two feet is more difficult than she imagined. In fact, once the novelty of being on her own wears off, she often finds the solid rock under her feet to be quite painful. The rigid world can seem harsh and cold. She may or may not yearn to return to the banks of the outer world temporarily. And parents should not discourage their daughters from doing this. In fact, temporarily returning to the coast is something that should be done throughout her adult life. By returning to the beaches, she will be able to revitalize and restore that spiritual and emotional playfulness that will make her stay in the outer world much more meaningful.

In addition to spiritually and emotionally returning to the coast, parents may find that their daughter is physically returning home. Often times parents find their brave and independent daughter suddenly showing up at their house for dinner every night. Or she will start coming home from college on the weekends, as I did. This is especially true if parents allowed their daughter to make a quick and easy exit in the beginning; if they supported her departure, she will feel comfortable in knowing that they will support her return. This is all quite normal, and like her jaunts to the beach, short trips back to the safety of her parent's house should not be discouraged. It is important that a young woman be able to physically return home if she is to strengthen her emotional and spiritual ties with her parents and younger siblings. It is also important for the emotional and spiritual well-being of every young woman to know that no matter how far away she travels, she will always be a part of the family.

In addition to the severing of ties, this third view is also defined by the knowledge that a young woman holds the power to modify what she sees. At this time she views the core as a world that needs to be altered. It is during this third viewpoint that a young woman's foundation becomes cluttered with soapboxes of all shapes and sizes. Her altruistic nature also has her contemplating some very serious social, environmental and political issues. Many times she will become so confused and disoriented by the many causes she has adopted that she loses track of what is truly important to her. Eventually, after she has fought for every conceivable cause, she will resign herself to the fact that the outer world is a place filled with imperfect situations and imperfect people who, just like herself, are simply trying to survive.

This realization, that the world doesn't have to be perfect in order to be divine, is what brings her to the fourth and final direction, which is one of tolerance. The fourth direction, which is really just a blink away from the third, stems from a young woman's need to change the world, but in a more succinct way. Again, she knows that she has the power to alter what she sees and she still holds the desire to soften the solid core, but she knows that a true wise-woman is one who is selective in how she uses her time and energy.

During these latter years of the seventh ritual she will also come to understand and appreciate her parent's wisdom, and will see them as companions instead of opponents. Her years as childbearer will be years of service, not only to her family, but to the world. In essence, it is her ability to embrace the world as it truly is and to be of service to it that finalizes the last ritual and sanctions her journey in getting there. These virtues of service and tolerance are truly the crowning pinnacles of womanhood and indeed the pinnacles of being human.

There are a few sharp drop-off points that come with living on this summit, though. The latter years of this ritual mark the time when a young woman first considers marrying and having children. And although these are certainly honorable duties, in her desire to give of her time and energy and herself, she often loses track of her own needs. Again, parents must gently remind their daughter that to be of service to the world doesn't mean *being* a servant. And being of use doesn't mean being used. Young women need to be reminded that one can hang onto their soulskin and still provide warmth to their mates and children. They also need to be told what to expect during their childbearing years, and what to expect during menopause. For only by knowing all of the spiritual transitions of womanhood, will they be able to prevent some of the hardships that these journeys entail.

After she has faced all four directions, and moved through all four viewpoints, the young woman will come to see that the hard center of the outer world is really just a solid mixture of her expectations, the expectations of others, and society as a whole. She will also learn that while her outer world appears to be a wholly different substance, it is really just the mirror image of her own divine nature manifested in a solid form and reversely arranged.

This principle, that the core of her outer life is just a hardened reflection of her inner life, is often a difficult concept for young women to grasp. In fact, it is a hard concept for even adult women who have lived many years in the outer world to comprehend. A simple way to understand it would be to compare the outer core to the looking-glass that Alice stepped through.

Mirrors themselves are solid substances made up of glass and painted with silver oxide to give the illusion of a wholly separate existence. But of course they don't contain a separate world. What we see when we look into them is merely our own reflection. The entire concept of Alice, who was able to move through the seemingly solid, rock-hard substance of glass that hung above her parent's fireplace and into a whimsical land, was based on the fact that she believed another world existed. She expected that she could step through this looking-glass to the other side, and so she did. Nevertheless, what she found in this make-believe land of the Red Queen and the White Queen was still simply a reflection of her own spirit. It is the same for the journeying adolescent girl. She believes in the existence of her parent's world, and so she makes the journey through her own mirror. But in the end, what she finds once she gets there is simply a mirror image of her own divine nature manifested from her own expectations and the expectations of those around her.

This metaphor, that the power and the beauty of her outer world is just a reflection of her inner world, has a mystical way of empowering and validating every young woman who hears it, and I believe it is one of the greatest spiritual truths that parents can share with their daughter. For this truth gives a young woman permission to look upon herself with the same amount of reverence and admiration that she had previously reserved for others. It also reminds her that she is ultimately responsible for what she finds through her own looking-glass.

And so this final revelation brings an end to the pilgrimage of adolescence. The inquisitive, delightful and sometimes exasperating young woman, having ventured through the mirror image of her spirit and travelled to the outer world, awakes to discover that a crown has been mysteriously placed upon her head. This crown, this golden circle of completion, is the manifestation of her own strength. It is a symbol of her ability to bear the weight of the world and of her ability to conquer her emotions and fears. And although it reflects her nobility, it also reflects her innate divinity as a vessel of creation in God's great design.

At first our Alice is surprised at her unexpected enthronement. But after moving around a bit, she discovers that the adornment fits quite well, almost as if it were custom made. She is delighted at having been bestowed such an honor, and continues her journey into her childbearing years with her head held high, her golden crown lighting the way. For she knows that to be chosen to walk upon the earth as a Spiritual Queen and Divine Mother is truly God's greatest gift of all.

The Menstrual Cycle: Honoring the Divine Dance of Creation

THE MENSTRUAL CYCLE is more than just a periodic anatomical occurrence. It is the divine way in which life expresses itself. Prompted by hormones and God's touch, it is the mixing of blood and spirit into a circular 28- to 30-day dance that transforms the female body from a mortal figure into a life-giving vessel. It is the way that the Goddess in every woman creates and prepares to give life, and creates and prepares to give life again and again. And the release of menstrual blood at the end of this cycle is an intricate part of the dance. It is the time when, at the end of creation, She rests. Like the Sabbath, the flow of the menstrual blood is a time for inner reflection and spiritual renewal. It is the time when women temporarily move from the outer world back into their inner world, and transitioning girls need to be reminded of this. They need to be taught that this monthly five to seven day span is not just an annoying interruption, but a spiritual intermission.

But getting this point across to young girls is not easy, especially in this day and age when manufacturers of women's products are advertising a hundred different ways for a woman to forget that she even has a period. And while tampons and some of the other modern products have certainly made life more convenient, they have also caused many women to be hypersensitive about the natural changes their bodies go through. That is why it is so important for parents to reiterate that the divine flow of menstrual blood is something to be honored, and celebrated—not something to be disregarded. And it is most assuredly not something to be embarrassed about.

I believe that the best way to overcome the negative views that society still holds of menstrual blood, is to continue to educate young girls about the natural changes of their cycles, and to do so in a voice and with a repetition that is even louder and more persistent than that of the advertising industry. Therefore, I have included a list of the reproductive organs that make up this divine dance of creation, along with a spiritual, more positive view of their functions. It is my hope that parents will incorporate these positive definitions into their ongoing conversations with their daughter.

Hypothalamus — This tiny gland in the limbic area of the brain (which is where emotions are controlled) is the conductor of the hormonal dance. It puts out other releasing hormones that, among other things, tell the pituitary gland when to start the dance or when to stimulate the ovaries and adrenals into producing sex hormones.

Pituitary Gland — This is the co-conductor of the hormonal dance. Also located in the limbic area of the brain, it sends out stimulating hormones that tell the ovaries and other glands what tune to play (or what hormone to make). The pituitary produces FSH (follicle stimulating hormone) during the first half of the menstrual cycle. FSH goes through the bloodstream to the ovary that will be ovulating that particular month and stimulates it into producing eggs. FSH also stimulates the production of estrogen. During the middle of the cycle the pituitary releases LH (luteinizing hormone) which causes an egg to burst from one of the ovaries.

Ovaries — The creator of life is, of course, God. But God's tools are the ovaries and testicles, for they are the glands that fashion and produce the seeds of life. They are the instruments upon which God plays the tune of Her creation. In looking at the pictures of the ovaries connected to the follicular tubes (the avenues through which the eggs move down into the uterus), one might even think they look like the hands of God, stretching down to touch the womb.

Uterus—Also referred to as the womb, the uterus is the sacred vessel of the divine as it exists on earth. It is the muscle that holds and embraces life as it forms and matures within the female body. It is no accident that this inverted pyramid also resembles a chalice, for it is the Grail that carries the wine of divinity for all mankind.

Eggs—These are the very seeds of life. They are the gems, the miracles of birth that God has entrusted to Her daughters. Female babies are born with approximately five million, give or take a million, immature eggs call "oocytes." Most of the seeds produce estrogen and then die off, but after a female has reached puberty, once a month one (or two) of them spring forth from the ovary and make the voyage down the fallopian tubes into the womb. The Goddess consciousness is stored in the memory of each of these eggs, and it is through these eggs that She dreams the world.

Estrogen—This is considered the main hormone of the female body because it is the most abundant of the sex hormones. It is made primarily in the ovaries, but it is also produced from androgens in the fat cells and adrenal glands. Estrogen is the juice of God's spirit that resides in every cell of a woman's body. It is the wine in the amulet that a journeying woman retrieves when she makes the trip back to her inner world, and it is the moist dew that refreshes her soulskin while she lives in the outer world.

Progesterone—This is the hormone that sustains the creative Goddess force in a woman's body. It comes from the word "gestate," which means "to bring forth." Progesterone is a calming hormone that relaxes and readies the womb to give birth to God's ideas (or children). It is the slow song that begins playing halfway through the woman's menstrual dance. At the end of the dance, if a woman has not conceived, the progesterone levels come to a crashing halt. This drop in progesterone and estrogen brings about the shedding of her uterine lining and menstrual flow. Progesterone is also a precursor to estrogen, which means it can be converted into estrogen if needed.

Testosterone—While found in considerably lower amounts in women than it is in men, testosterone is still very important to the structure of a woman's hormonal dance. This hormone is the get up and go that moves a woman through her cycle, and it is the steady beat of the drum that keeps the rhythm of the other hormones in tune.

THE MENARCHE
TREASURE CHEST

There is a special box that sits on the top shelf of my closet. It is a treasure chest of sorts that I have been saving for years. Occasionally I pull it down and add another cherished item to the collection inside, but mainly it stays hidden, as I wait for the all-important and, as of yet, undetermined date for its unveiling—the day my daughter starts her first period.

I began putting this treasure chest together after I had a hard time deciding which gift would be appropriate to give Amanda on this special day. There were so many things I wanted to tell her about, so many things I wanted to share with her about my own journey through womanhood. One or two items weren't enough. So I decided to put together a collection, a treasure chest, to be opened the minute her ethereal barge meets with the outer world.

On the outside of the box are pink, blue and yellow butterflies. Packed neatly inside is a representation of what I believe to be the essential items of womanhood. Some of these things are merely reminders of my daughter's maiden years— security blankets to hold as she adjusts to life on the beaches of the outer world. Some of the other items are passports to use as she journeys through the roads inland. Others still are the band-aids that she will need after she has made those inevitable tumbles on the hardened inner core. And then there are simple items that represent the everyday physical necessities that go with being female.

I believe this box is unique, not only because it represents one girl's journey, but because it contains dated material. Much like a time capsule, over the years it can be reopened and looked at again and again by generations to come. Although few of us received gifts like this when we started our periods, it is my wish that the menarche treasure chest becomes a time-honored tradition that all girls enjoy. I can only imagine how wonderful it would have been to have received a box that contained a sampling of what my great-grandmother Ruby considered to be symbolic of her womanhood. Hopefully, my great-granddaughter won't have to imagine, for she will have this gift, along with the items that her own mother and grandmother (my daughter) have added.

While I have intentionally *not* revealed the specific contents of my daughter's menarche box—I want it to be sacred, something that is shared between just the two of us—following are some items to consider when putting together a menarche treasure chest for a transitioning girl:

Stones or crystals—A pink moonstone (also known as bloodstone), a birthstone, or any type of crystal.

Books—There are many to choose from, but my favorites are: Marianne Williamson's *A Woman's Worth*, Gloria Steinheim's *Self-Esteem*, Iyanla Vanzant's *Don't Give it Away*, Steven Carter and Julia Solol's *What Smart Women Know*, Christiane Northrup's *Women's Bodies, Women's Wisdom*, and Erica Jong's *How to Save Your Own Life*.

Poetry—By famous poets or handwritten by parents. One of my favorites for young women is called *After a While*, by Veronica A. Shoffstall.

Jewelry—A moon charm or necklace, or a family heirloom.

Photographs—Childhood pictures, or photographs of a favorite female relative.

Clothing—A sexy bra or garter, a scarf, or an embroidered handkerchief. Silk or dried flowers, wedding or christening flowers, or a simple red rose.

Letters—Love letters, or a note to your daughter or future granddaughter.

Miscellaneous items—A panty liner, a band-aid cut in the shape of a heart, red nail polish, a hair net or ribbon.

In addition to carefully choosing what to put inside the treasure chest, it is equally important to carefully choose what to put on the outside. In fact, decorating the box itself is a very important ritual, as it represents a girl's external, outer world nature. I chose a box covered with colorful butterflies because it was symbolic of what I hope will be my daughter's carefree and spirited journey through the childbearing years. The treasure chest itself doesn't have to be elaborate, though. It might even be a container that has some special meaning in and of itself, such as a grandmother's sewing basket.

Some ideas for decorating the outside of the treasure chest are:

- Make a collage of photographs and glue them to the top.

- Decorate the box in the journeying girl's favorite theme.

- Paint or draw cycles of the moon on its cover.

- Wrap the box in a newspaper from the day the journeying girl was born.

- Wrap the box in plain white paper and then start a tradition in which each girl who receives the box signs her name on it.

RITUALS FOR CELEBRATING THE START OF THE MENSTRUAL CYCLE

A girl's period, or moon cycle, is a momentousness occasion. It symbolizes the beginning of her years as childbearer and of bearer of the world. And it also marks the moment when she first connects with the outer world and becomes a vessel of creation. Although she will not want to be creating life until she is much older, she officially becomes anointed with the life giving elixir the moment she starts her first period.

The celebration of a girl's first menstrual cycle doesn't have to be elaborate. In fact, most girls prefer to have something smaller with only their closest friends involved. The party can have a light, carefree atmosphere where mother and daughter go to lunch, or it can take on a more sacred, serious mood with the use of candles, sacred ceremonies and lots of guests. The most important thing to remember is that the transitioning girl needs to be involved in the planning of her own party, and its theme should be her choice.

Although the actually timing of the event is something that will have to be announced at the last minute, the theme of the menarche celebration itself can be planned in advance. In fact, it is wise for parents to start talking with their daughter about the kind of celebration that she wants right around the time that they first speak with her about menstruation. That way the positive, celebrated aspects of what it means to be a woman can be reinforced.

Following are examples and themes that parents may want to use for their daughter's menarche celebration:

CASUAL: The celebration of menarche doesn't have to include a lot of people to be memorable. Sometimes spending time with a parent, or going out to lunch, can be just as important to a transitioning girl. This lunch can include something impromptu such as going to the mall to pick out a new outfit, or signing up for an art class together.

MODERN: The contemporary menarche celebration tends to include only friends that are about the same age as the transitioning girl, and its theme is usually light. In fact, in many respects it resembles a conventional birthday party. The ceremony itself can consist of inviting friends over for pizza or going out to a special restaurant or movie. It can be an all-night sleepover party or last only an hour or two. Although the occasion for the celebration should be mentioned at the onset, no formal ceremony or reading needs to be done.

FORMAL: Conventional menarche celebrations are more structured and elaborate than the casual and modern party. They take a lot more planning and forethought, and often have to be put off until at least a month or two from the actual date that a girl has her first period. But the time and effort that go into planning this type of commemoration is usually worth the wait. Like the less formal celebrations, these elaborate parties can take on any form or theme that the transitioning girl wants. Below is an example of a formal ceremony that a transitioning girl might want to use:

The guests of this type of conventional menarche celebration should be of all ages, and should dress according to their status. Maidens—girls who have not yet started their period—should wear white. Women who are of childbearing age should wear red. And women who are postmenopausal should wear black to signify that they have mastered the mysteries of life.

The ceremony itself consists of three segments: the storytelling, the declaration and the initiation. It commences with a white candle being lit and given to the transitioning girl, and all the guests sitting in a circle around her. Each guest who is either of childbearing age or postmenopausal, should share the story of their first period. If they can't remember or would not like to share their story, they can relate what being a woman means to them or recount a story that they feel is appropriate to the occasion.

After each guest has been given a chance to speak, the declaration begins.

The declaration is that part of the celebration in which the mother or older relative of the transitioning girl reads a prepared statement declaring the girl a childbearer. The declaration can be a poem, a prayer or a few simple statements about being a woman. An example of a declaration might be: "We welcome you Amanda into the circle of women. You are now a member of the woman's moon lodge, in mind, body and spirit. We bless you on your journey into the childbearing years. May your monthly bleeding be a time of joy and reverence for your body. And may its cyclic nature remind you that your power to heal and to love are never-ending."

The final segment of the menarche ritual is the initiation. The initiation signifies the starting of the menstrual cycle, where the elements of the inner world—water/emotion and fire/spirit—meet with those of the outer world—air/mental and earth/physical. The mixing of these elements can be celebrated in many ways. The best and easiest method is to simply have these elements displayed prominently at the ceremony: A candle for spirit, a bowl of water for emotion, and a sprinkling of dirt for physical. During the initiation, the white candle that the transitioning girl is holding should be exchanged for a red candle and lit by the one or all of the guests who are of childbearing age. Gifts may also be exchanged at this time. These gifts can be something that represents a girl's passage into womanhood, such as red beads (or other jewelry), a red flower or other symbol of nature. Or they can be something that represents the outer world, such as an article of clothing (earth) or a magazine subscription (air).

The ceremony can end with a song or drumming, or the reading of an additional poem or declaration. Again, it is important to remember that the ceremony should be personalized to meet the wants and needs of the transitioning girl. It should be something that she should look back on as a marker of her first steps as a childbearer.

Glossary

Adrenal Glands—Two glands located just above the kidneys that produce hormones and control stress.

Androgens—Although considered to be male hormones, androgens have a very significant role in the female body. They are responsible for a woman's libido, muscle strength, and overall sense of well-being.

Barge—The ethereal vessel that symbolizes a girl's ability to transport herself through any crises. In this book it represents the strength that a girl uses to transport herself from her own inner world to the outer world.

Childbearing Years—The period of time in which a woman is able to bear children. It also denotes the time in which a girl is spiritually mature enough to bear the world.

Estrogen—A hormone secreted primarily by the ovaries, adrenal glands, testicles and fat cells. The three major types of estrogen are estradiol, estrone and estriol. Estradiol is the estrogen that is produced by a woman's ovaries, and is the strongest and most active of the three. Estriol is the estrogen that a woman's body produces during pregnancy. Estrone is made from estradiol and is stored in a woman's fat cells, and is the least, or weakest, of the three estrogens.

Follicular Phase—The first half, or first two weeks, of a woman's menstrual cycle. During this stage, the uterus is building up its lining in preparation for the egg that is about to be released from the ovary.

FSH—Follicle Stimulating Hormone. Produced during the first half of the menstrual cycle by the pituitary gland, FSH moves through the bloodstream to the ovary and stimulates it into producing eggs. FSH also stimulates the production of estrogen.

Hypothalamus—A gland in the limbic area of the brain that puts out the releasing hormone that tells the pituitary gland when to stimulate the ovaries into production.

Inner World—An internal existence where the majority of little girls live before puberty, and where the majority of women retreat to when they go through menopause. Being in the inner world means being present in the inner, spiritual world of one's being.

Initiation—The onset or beginning of a new experience. During an adolescent girl's journey, she is often initiated into society through a series of rites, or rituals, right around the time she starts her period.

LH—Luteinizing hormone. It is produced mainly by the pituitary gland and is released during the second half of a woman's menstrual cycle. The secretion of this hormone is responsible for the egg bursting forth from the ovary.

Luteal Phase—The second half, or two weeks, of a woman's menstrual cycle. It is the time, after ovulation, when progesterone is preparing the lining of the uterus. If no egg was fertilized, then the lining will be shed.

Menarche—Typically used to describe a woman's first menstrual cycle. But it also denotes the journey through puberty.

Menopause—Typically used to describe a woman's last menstrual cycle, but it also denotes a woman's journey through the final years of menstruation.

Menses—The menstrual flow or discharge of menstrual blood.

Outer World—An external existence where women find themselves spending the majority of their childbearing years. Being in the outer world means being an active participant in the comings and goings of the physical world.

Ovaries—The two female reproductive glands that produce eggs and hormones.

Pilgrimage—A spiritual journey.

Pituitary Gland—Located in the limbic area of the brain, it sends out the stimulating hormones that tells the ovaries what hormones to produce.

Progesterone—Derived from the word "gestate," which means to "bring forth." The hormone is produced during the second half of the menstrual cycle, and it prepares the uterus for the fertilized egg. It is also what sustains the lining of the uterus during pregnancy.

Rite—A sacred or ceremonial act.

Soulskin—The sacred covering of a woman's spirit that protects her from harm in the outer world.

Testosterone—A hormone that is made by the ovaries, adrenal glands, and testes. Although found primarily in men, women's bodies also make and depend on testosterone to build muscle, and for an overall sense of well-being.

Waning—To decrease in size. During the lunar cycle it represents the last quarter when the light of the moon is decreasing. During a woman's menstrual cycle, it represents the luteal phase, or the time after ovulation and before her menses.

Waxing—The molding or making of something. It represents the first half of the lunar cycle when the moon is becoming full. It also represents the first two weeks of a woman's menstrual cycle, or the follicular phase, when her uterus is building up its lining before ovulation.

THE SEVEN SACRED RITES OF MENOPAUSE

BY KRISTI MEISENBACH BOYLAN

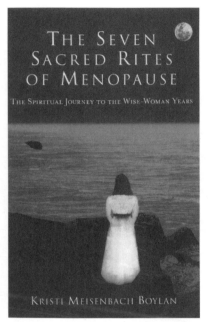

Menopause is much more than just a list of physical ailments, menopause is a spiritual journey.

Kristi Meisenbach Boylan outlines the seven rituals that menpausal women move through on their voyage to the wise-woman years.

Learn why these seven ceremonial milestones should be viewed as celebrations, not as symptoms of illness or disease.

"The Seven Sacred Rites of Menopause *speaks directly to a woman's soul. It's a book that every woman who is either preparing to enter menopause, or is going through menopause, will want to read for guidance and illumination. Kristi Meisenbach Boylan has provided a menopausal roadmap for generations to come.*"
— Marianne Williamson, author of
A Return to Love and *Imagine*

$11.95
1-800-784-9553

Blues for Bird
by Martin Gray
288 pages $16.95

The Book of Good Habits
*Simple and Creative Ways to
Enrich Your Life*
by Dirk Mathison
224 pages $9.95

Café Nation
Coffee Folklore, Magick, and Divination
by Sandra Mizumoto Posey
224 pages $9.95

Collecting Sins
A Novel
by Steven Sobel
288 pages $13

**Free Stuff and Good Deals for
Folks over 50**
by Linda Bowman
240 pages $12.95

Free Stuff and Good Deals for Your Pet
by Linda Bowman
240 pages $12.95

Free Stuff and Good Deals on the Internet
by Linda Bowman
240 pages $12.95

Health Care Handbook
*A Consumer's Guide to the American Health
Care System*
by Mark Cromer
256 pages $12.95

Helpful Household Hints
The Ultimate Guide to Housekeeping
by June King
224 pages $12.95

**How to Find Your Family Roots and Write
Your Family History**
by William Latham and Cindy Higgins
288 pages $14.95

How to Speak Shakespeare
by Cal Pritner and Louis Colaianni
144 pages $16.95

**How to Win Lotteries, Sweepstakes,
and Contests in the 21st Century**
by Steve "America's Sweepstakes King" Ledoux
224 pages $14.95

The Keystone Kid
Tales of Early Hollywood
by Coy Watson, Jr.
304 pages $24.95

Letter Writing Made Easy!
*Featuring Sample Letters for Hundreds of
Common Occasions*
by Margaret McCarthy
224 pages $12.95

Letter Writing Made Easy! Volume 2
*Featuring More Sample Letters for Hundreds
of Common Occasions*
by Margaret McCarthy
224 pages $12.95

Nancy Shavick's Tarot Universe
by Nancy Shavick
336 pages $15.95

Offbeat Food
Adventures in an Omnivorous World
by Alan Ridenour
240 pages $19.95

Offbeat Golf
A Swingin' Guide To a Worldwide Obsession
by Bob Loeffelbein
192 pages $17.95

Offbeat Marijuana
*The Life and Times of the World's
Grooviest Plant*
by Saul Rubin
240 pages $19.95

Offbeat Museums
*The Collections and Curators of America's
Most Unusual Museums*
by Saul Rubin
240 pages $19.95

Past Imperfect
*How Tracing Your Family Medical History
Can Save Your Life*
by Carol Daus
240 pages $12.95

Quack!
*Tales of Medical Fraud from the Museum of
Questionable Medical Devices*
by Bob McCoy
240 pages $19.95

The Seven Sacred Rites of Menarche
The Spiritual Journey of the Adolescent Girl
by Kristi Meisenbach Boylan
160 pages $11.95

The Seven Sacred Rites of Menopause
The Spiritual Journey to the Wise-Woman Years
by Kristi Meisenbach Boylan
144 pages $11.95

Silent Echoes
*Discovering Early Hollywood Through the Films
of Buster Keaton*
by John Bengtson
240 pages $24.95

What's Buggin' You?
Michael Bohdan's Guide to Home Pest Control
by Michael Bohdan
256 pages $12.95

ORDER FORM

	Quantity	Amount
Blues for Bird ($16.95)		
The Book of Good Habits ($9.95)		
Café Nation ($9.95)		
Collecting Sins ($13)		
Free Stuff and Good Deals for Folks over 50 ($12.95)		
Free Stuff and Good Deals for Your Pet ($12.95)		
Free Stuff and Good Deals on the Internet ($12.95)		
Health Care Handbook ($12.95)		
Helpful Household Hints ($12.95)		
How to Find Your Family Roots . . . ($14.95)		
How to Speak Shakespeare ($16.95)		
How to Win Lotteries, Sweepstakes, and Contests . . . ($14.95)		
The Keystone Kid ($24.95)		
Letter Writing Made Easy! ($12.95)		
Letter Writing Made Easy! Volume 2 ($12.95)		
Nancy Shavick's Tarot Universe ($15.95)		
Offbeat Food ($19.95)		
Offbeat Golf ($17.95)		
Offbeat Marijuana ($19.95)		
Offbeat Museums ($19.95)		
Past Imperfect ($12.95)		
Quack! ($19.95)		
The Seven Sacred Rites of Menarche ($11.95)		
The Seven Sacred Rites of Menopause ($11.95)		
Silent Echoes ($24.95)		
What's Buggin' You? ($12.95)		

Shipping & Handling:

1 book $3.00
Each additional book is $ .50

Subtotal _____

CA residents add 8% sales tax _____

Shipping and Handling (see left) _____

TOTAL _____

Name _____

Address _____

City _____ State _____ Zip _____

☐ Visa ☐ MasterCard   Card No.: _____

Exp. Date _____ Signature _____

☐ Enclosed is my check or money order payable to:

Santa Monica Press LLC
P.O. Box 1076
Santa Monica, CA 90406
www.santamonicapress.com

1-800-784-9553